Confident
Web Design

Confident
Web Design

Master the fundamentals
of website creation and
supercharge your career

Kenny Wood

First published in Great Britain and the United States in 2020 by Kogan Page Limited
Reissued in 2020.

2nd Floor, 45 Gee Street	Martin P Hill Consulting	4737/23 Ansari Road
London	122 W 27th Street	Daryaganj
EC1V 3RS	New York, NY 10001	New Delhi 110002
United Kingdom	USA	India

www.koganpage.com

Kogan Page books are printed on paper from sustainable forests.

© Kenny Wood 2018 and 2020

The right of Kenny Wood to be identified as the author of this work has been asserted by him in accordance with the Copyright, Designs and Patents Act 1988.

ISBNs

Hardback	978 1 78966 347 1
Paperback	978 1 78966 345 7
Ebook	978 1 78966 346 4

British Library Cataloguing-in-Publication Data

A CIP record for this book is available from the British Library.

Library of Congress Control Number

2020941854

Typeset by Integra Software Services, Pondicherry
Print production managed by Jellyfish
Printed and bound in Great Britain by CPI Group (UK) Ltd, Croydon CR0 4YY

To my partner and children, Melody, Indigo and Nirvana, who provided the source of inspiration to become the man I am.

ACKNOWLEDGEMENTS

My thanks and appreciation to my loving partner Melody who provided me with endless support and encouragement throughout the writing of this book.

To my beautiful children who saw me sacrifice my time with them in exchange for the words contained in this text.

To my caring sister Laura for her eagle-eyed review of the text and for her words of encouragement throughout.

And to all of my family and friends for the encouragement and excitement that they afforded me throughout course of the journey.

To you all I am forever grateful.

CONTENTS

PART THREE JavaScript 155

Introduction

Web design is full of creativity, fun, progression and skill. It is an ever-evolving subject that is hugely satisfying to learn and master. Learning how to develop websites provides a person with far more than an understanding of how to write code. It develops them as a person; it teaches them how to think for themselves, solve problems, be resilient in the face of seemingly impossible challenges and think outside of the box.

Every challenge we face when building a website furthers our understanding of both the field and of ourselves. Once you have finished working your way through this book, you will find that not only do you look at websites in a completely different way, you might just look at yourself differently too. Web design is hugely satisfying and is an industry full of developers who don't just love what they do, they live and breathe it.

If you work your way through this book, I guarantee that you too will learn to love programming and all of its quirks. I am a computer programmer with 12 years of experience and every day I still wake up thirsty to learn more about the subject. I often dream in code and I look at the world in an extremely logical and functional way that allows me to complete any task that I set my mind to with control and understanding. Web design has fuelled my thirst for knowledge and understanding and continues to be my true first love. Web design is far more than just programming – it is a huge part of many people's lives and soon, you too will be one of those people.

Good luck working your way through this book. I am sure you will have a thoroughly enjoyable time working through the exercises, learning more about the field, before finally building your very own website at the end. This book aims to challenge you – possibly in ways that you've never been challenged before. It will also require you to think in ways you probably haven't thought before. At times it will be difficult, at times frustrating and at other times downright infuriating, but I urge you to stick with it, to accept the challenges you face, and overcome them with patience and resilience. Learning to become a web developer is also a process of learning how to learn and how to problem solve. These skills will serve you well in whatever you choose to do after the book is finished.

Now, let's learn how to build websites.

01
How the web works: tools and languages of web design

What we will learn in this chapter

Before we dive into learning how websites are built, we need to understand the landscape in which a website operates. In this chapter, you will discover exactly what we mean when we use the term World Wide Web. We will then explore exactly what happens every time you visit a webpage, and how that webpage reaches you. Even if you are already familiar with how the World Wide Web works, it is always important to recap the essentials before starting to learn web design.

This chapter will then teach you about the essential tools used in modern web design, providing some examples of the recommended versions of these tools that are the most widely adopted across the web development landscape. The web development landscape is an ever-evolving environment, with constantly changing requirements and best practices. As such, the world of web development comprises an abundance of ever-changing tools and workflows to assist the modern web developer. While there is no shortage of tools and software that a web developer can use, there is a very small number of resources actually required in order to get your website up and running.

We will then break down the languages that are used on the web and explain their role in creating a website. You will learn the difference between front-end development and back-end development and explore the languages that fall into each category. We will also look at where CMSs (content management systems) fit into this spectrum and their role in the web development landscape.

The key principles on which the World Wide Web functions

The internet

The internet is a global network of connected devices. This network contains many other networks within it, which connect the millions of devices that exist at various points around the world. Devices on the network can communicate with one another and exchange information over a multitude of languages, known as protocols.

The World Wide Web

The World Wide Web ('the web') is a method of accessing information across the internet using a protocol named HTTP (Hypertext Transfer Protocol). The World Wide Web is an information-sharing platform built on top of the internet, which allows the devices across the network to communicate freely in a common language. HTTP is one of many protocols used across the internet. (Another example is SMTP, which is used for email communication.)

Webpages

Webpages are written using HTML (Hypertext Markup Language), then saved and uploaded to a web server, which will host the files ready for another device on the network to view upon request (using the HTTP protocol).

Browsers

A browser is a computer program capable of interpreting and displaying HTML files for the user to view and interact with. The most common browsers today are:

- Firefox;
- Internet Explorer;
- Opera;
- Google Chrome;
- Safari.

Servers

A server is simply a computer on the network, which has the sole purpose of serving webpages or files to other devices across the network upon request. Servers are discoverable via IP addresses.

Domains

A domain is a bit like an address or a postcode. It tells the browser where to look for a file. Effectively, a domain is a name for a server on the network. Anything after the forward slash tells the browser which file on that server you are looking for.

Subdomains

A subdomain is used to divide your website up into smaller sections. For example, we could set bookings.example.com to go to a different server from the one used for www.example.com.

URLs

A URL is a location on the network where a particular resource exists. The resource could be anything from a webpage, to an image or a video. Typically a URL is formed out of the segments shown in Figure 1.1.

1.1

DNS

A DNS is a network of servers, which are responsible for looking up the IP address associated with the domain specified. In this respect, they operate a bit like a phone book; you pass them the domain name and they return the IP address of the server you are requesting access to.

Putting it all together

Let's walk through exactly what happens every time you visit a webpage via your browser:

1 User enters URL into the browser (for example www.example.com).
2 Browser looks up the domain name on DNS server.
3 Browser obtains IP address of file server from the DNS server.
4 Browser requests file from the server on the found IP address.
5 Server returns requested file to browser.
6 Browser displays file to user.

Exercise

Go to http://mxtoolbox.com/DNSLookup.aspx and test out searching for various domains. Have a look at some of the IP addresses associated with that domain. Test what happens when you put that IP address directly into your URL bar on your browser. Notice how the domain is simply a name for the IP address of the server. By doing this exercise, you are effectively replicating the first steps that the browser takes whenever you visit a webpage.

The tools and languages of web design

In this book, we will be focusing on the front-end spectrum of the landscape. We will be learning about HTML, CSS and JavaScript, before using these tools to build a webpage. These front-end languages are comprehensive enough to allow us to build a static website with interactive elements that could be used for a number of different scenarios.

Table 1.1 Tools and languages glossary

Static website	A static website is a website that has content that does not change dynamically. It is not connected to a database, and as such the information is written directly into the HTML and will not change unless the web developer changes it manually by altering the code
Languages	In computer programming terms a 'language' is a set of defined commands, used as a method of giving instructions to a computer
Remote server	A server that is not directly accessible to a user physically, usually located in another building and sometimes in another location entirely

(continued)

Table 1.1 (Continued)

FTP	File Transfer Protocol – a standard network protocol used for transferring data between a client and a server
Debugging	The process of locating and removing errors from our website

With a knowledge of HTML, CSS and JavaScript, you could learn an easy-to-use CMS, such as WordPress, and create dynamic websites for any situation.

Tools

Text editor

A website is written in a number of different text-based languages, such as HTML, CSS and JavaScript.

In order to write these languages that will be interpreted by the computer, we need to use a text editor. There are many different text editors available for use in web design. While the reality is that you could write a website using nothing more than the standard notepad application included with all installations of Microsoft Windows, this would not be ideal for your website as you wouldn't be benefiting from the additional features that come with a highly specialized text editor, purpose-built for computer programming.

A relatively new text editor that has quickly become something of an industry standard is Sublime Text (https://www.sublimetext.com/). Sublime Text is a free application (albeit with an option to pay to remove an infrequent reminder popup), and it is full of features that make it perfect for web development – including the ability to install plugins to improve your programming experience.

We will be using Sublime Text throughout this book, and introducing some power-user tips throughout to help you to get the most out of the software. While you do not have to use Sublime Text, it is recommended that you use it for the duration of this book as it will give you an understanding of how text editors are used in web development and also some of the plugins that are most commonly used. This understanding of how to enhance your experience of using a text editor, along with an awareness of the most useful and popular plugins, can then be taken over and used on any other plugin-based text editor you wish to use going forward, such as Brackets or Atom.

FTP client

As I explained earlier, websites are hosted on web servers. Because web servers are (mostly) remote servers, we need a way to communicate with the web server and deploy our website files to it.

For this we use an FTP (File Transfer Protocol) client. An FTP client is an application that allows you to transfer files between your computer and a remote computer (in this case, our server) via the FTP. Effectively an FTP client allows us to connect to the server and then move files to and from it, just as you would a folder on your own hard drive.

As with text editors, there are many different variants of FTP clients that can be used, but we will be using free software that is widely adopted across the landscape called FileZilla. FileZilla works on both Windows and Mac and supports a wide array of features, though in this book we will only be using the base features required for us to get our website online, such as connecting to servers, transferring files and setting permissions.

Browser

Simply put, web browsers are responsible for presenting the websites that we build. For the end user, this is the main role of their web browser so they are generally happy with any of the modern web browsers that are available. However, for a web developer, there is more to consider when selecting a web browser. When developing for the web, we need a method of debugging our code and inspecting exactly what is going on.

As such, modern web browsers contain a mode that most end-users will never use and are mostly unaware of, responsible for the debugging of the website. Each browser has its own version of a debugger, mostly referred to as the 'inspector' or 'inspector tools'. This mode is where a web developer will be spending most of their time when debugging their website in the browser and, as such, is a huge influencer when deciding which browser to use.

Once again, we will be using the most widely adopted browser for web developers, which is Google Chrome. Chrome has a fantastic set of developer tools at its disposal, which are invaluable to the modern developer.

It is important to note that each web browser has its own set of rules and standards for displaying content, which means that a website will render differently in each browser. As such, we must install and test our website in the current most popular web browsers to ensure that our website renders correctly.

Currently the most popular web browsers, as mentioned previously, are:

- Google Chrome;
- Firefox;
- Safari;
- Internet Explorer;
- Opera.

We should therefore aim to install and test our websites on all of these popular browsers.

Image editor (optional)

The modern web is a very visual medium. Where websites once had to use images sparingly, if at all, owing to slow internet connection speeds, with the vast improvements made to internet speed over the past decade, websites can now justify including a lot of media and don't have to worry as much about their page loading speed. Search for the 2005 BBC homepage and compare it to the same site just five years later in 2010. Web technology advances every single day, which is what makes being a web developer such an exciting career. With this recent trend towards particularly media-rich websites, housing a lot of images and video, it is important that we are able to create and manipulate media for use on our website.

A common tool for the modern web developer is an image editor. While this is not completely essential, it is highly recommended. An image editor has many uses for a web developer: it allows us to crop, resize, edit and optimize images for the web. This allows us to have much more control over the media used on our website and, in turn, helps us to build a better website.

Free options for professional image editors are limited, though they do exist. GIMP, for example, is a cross-platform image editor which is more than up to the task of manipulating images for the web – though it is far from being the most widely used tool for image manipulation in web design. That title belongs to Adobe Photoshop. Photoshop is a brilliant tool that has been used by web developers for many years. With fantastic image optimization settings, it allows us to create website-ready graphics with relative ease. Photoshop offers a free trial, which will allow you to test out the software for 30 days.

Photoshop is not essential for you to complete this book as the assets will be provided for you ready for use. However, it is still recommended that you read the Photoshop section closely to understand why image editors are used in web development.

Exercise

Before we can progress, we must ensure that we are working in the same, or a very similar, environment. As such, at a minimum you need to install the following applications on to your computer:

- Sublime Text;

- FileZilla; and

- Google Chrome.

Optionally (but highly recommended) you can install the following:

- Adobe Photoshop;

- Firefox;

- Safari;

- Internet Explorer

- Opera.

If you are working on a Mac (and so using macOS), you will be unable to install Internet Explorer as a native app on your machine. While in this book it is not essential for you to have Internet Explorer installed in order to progress through the course, in the real world you will still need to test in Internet Explorer so you will need a way of accessing your website using this particular browser. One method of doing this is by using the Remote Desktop application and virtual machines to test using Internet Explorer on a Windows instance. You can find out more about this on the Microsoft Internet Explorer blog page: https://blogs.msdn.microsoft.com/ie/2014/11/02/announcing-remoteie-test-the-latest-ie-on-windows-mac-os-x-ios-and-android.

Languages of web design

Front-end vs back-end

You may have heard the terms 'front-end' and 'back-end' when discussing web development. These terms are used to describe the two different aspects of the programming of a website. Front-end is responsible for creating everything that a user sees and interacts with in their browser, while back-end concerns itself more with the information itself and generating dynamic information that the front-end then displays. Let's break this down in more detail below.

Front-end

In a nutshell, the front-end is everything that the user sees. This includes the design of the site, but also how the user interacts with the site. Popups, input fields, buttons and menus are all front-end components that would be built by a front-end web developer. The front-end uses a small number of languages to achieve these results. They are as follows:

HTML

HTML (HyperText Markup Language) is the one of the main languages in web design. It is the code that is interpreted by your browser and tells your browser what to display. HTML is not a programming language, but a 'markup language'. HTML is used for describing your webpage: it tells the browser what is a heading, what is a paragraph, what is an image, what is a list and so on. It simply describes and breaks up your content. HTML elements are the building blocks of your website.

CSS

CSS (Cascading Style Sheets) is responsible for describing to your browser how the HTML elements should be displayed. CSS defines how everything appears. It defines colours, sizes, positions and much more. CSS can be very powerful and can change the whole look of a website in just one line of code.

JavaScript

JavaScript is a programming language that runs in the browser. It is responsible for adding interaction to webpages. JavaScript is the only true programming language that can be interpreted and executed by a browser, meaning JavaScript is the only way of giving programming instructions to the browser. JavaScript is commonly used to manipulate the elements defined in your HTML. Some typical examples of how JavaScript is used in web design are as follows: checking form entries are valid before submitting the form, updating content on a click of a button, and triggering popups.

Back-end

Back-end development concerns itself with more behind-the-scenes logic. In its simplest form, back-end development comprises a server and a database. The code that the back-end developer writes will execute on the server, rather than in the browser. The back-end developer will also be responsible for the database, which is where the website data is stored. For the sake of simplicity, think of a database as a big spreadsheet, which can be accessed and have information pulled from it at will to be given to the front-end to display. The back-end is responsible for storing the information given to it by the front-end. Forms you complete on a website, for example, will be handled by the back-end and stored in a database.

Languages

There are many different languages that can be used on the back-end, such as Java, PHP, .NET, Ruby, Python, Perl and many more. Each of these languages is dynamic and they all run directly on the server and do not interact in any way with the browser. Each language is described as a 'scripting language' as files are written as scripts which are then run on the server and return an output. Effectively a script is a series of instructions for the computer/server to carry out in a specific order.

CMS

You may have heard about CMSs (Content Management Systems) such as WordPress, Joomla, Drupal, etc. These systems bridge the gap between front-end and back-end; they run on the server and are written using a back-end language (typically PHP). However, they allow a front-end developer to carry out typically back-end functions by using an interface that runs in the browser. For example, a CMS will allow a front-end developer to easily store and read information from a database and output it using front-end languages such as HTML, CSS and JavaScript.

What we have learned in this chapter

We have learned the technical difference between the internet and the World Wide Web. We have explored exactly what a webpage actually is and briefly introduced the main construction language of web design (HTML). We also explored the most popular web browsers and looked at the intricate connection between servers, domains, subdomains, URLs and IP addresses. We then learned the role the DNS plays in that connection and then put everything together to understand what is happening every time we visit a webpage, and just how that webpage reaches our web browser. You should now have a base understanding of the key principles that underline how the World Wide Web works, which will form the foundation for the rest of this book.

In this chapter we also learned about the modern web landscape and the essential tools used to create some of the web experiences we see on a daily basis. We explored why it is important to install more than one web browser, and understood some of the benefits of using a specialized text editor for web design. We introduced FTP clients and touched upon why it is important for a web developer to use an image editing application.

You should now also understand the difference between the front-end and the back-end and have an understanding of the languages that reside on either side of the spectrum. We looked at how CMSs fit into that landscape and their role in the web industry. We also introduced the main languages used in front-end web development and their role within the browser.

Part One
HTML

In this section we will be learning how to code using the HTML markup language. On this journey we will be building the HTML structure of our website and introducing the various tags that form the makeup of the HTML language and modern webpages. We will introduce best practices and ways of working that will enable you to write high-quality code that could be used in a production environment.

This journey through the use of HTML will see us tackling the anatomy of the tags that form the makeup of the HTML language, before looking at how we use these tags to render text, hyperlinks, images, tables, lists and forms. These elements form the basis of all webpages, and learning how to use them will empower you to be able to create an abundance of diverse and interesting structures for your website.

Each chapter will introduce new concepts that we will be putting into practice. Each concept will follow on from and build upon the previous one, so it is important that you carry out each activity before moving on to the next concept, in order to ensure that you are always working from the same codebase as the book. The chapters will expect you to follow the code examples, and write the same, or in some cases very similar, code in your text editor in order to put into practice what is being taught in each section. At the end of this

HTML section, you will have the shell of your website built, ready to be styled using CSS in the subsequent section.

Some of the section exercises will require additional files, which can be downloaded from **http://indigomelody.com/confident-web-design/files**. This folder contains subfolders for each chapter, which will contain both the assets required for the exercise and an example of the desired outcome from the exercise. You should compare your code to that of the example after each section to ensure you have achieved the outcome of the activity.

02
HTML Part 1

What we will learn in this chapter

This chapter will cover the basics of understanding HTML, as well as tags, text, links, images, tables and lists.

HTML

HTML basics

Let's first introduce HTML again in slightly more detail. We know already that HTML is the language responsible for explaining our content and webpage structure to the web browser for it to interpret and display to the end user; now let's explore just how that works.

An HTML page is formed of many different HTML elements. Elements are represented by tags. A tag is a piece of code that we wrap around our content to describe what type of content it is; it is effectively a label for our content. We might use a tag to explain to the browser that our snippet of text is a header, or a paragraph, or even a bullet point list.

These tags are interpreted by the browser, but not displayed to the end user. They are simply used to tell the browser what the content is and therefore how to display it.

HTML tags

Let's break down the anatomy of an HTML tag. HTML tags typically come in pairs: an opening tag and a closing tag. The first tag tells the browser where our element starts and the second tag tells it where our content ends. We call these tags the 'opening tag' and the 'closing tag', and they have slightly different syntaxes.

Table 2.1   HTML glossary

HTML elements	The building blocks of an HTML page, it is an individual component of the HTML document, which usually houses some content of some form
Metadata	Metadata is data that describes other data

```
<tag>content</tag>
```

Let's see some examples of how these tags are used in the wild, looking at two examples where we use tags to mark up text. We will explore this in more detail later in the chapter.

```
<h1>Header Text</h1>
<p>Paragraph Text</p>
```

You will notice how the opening tag is merely a word contained in angled brackets, while the ending tag is the same, but with a forward slash after the opening angled bracket. Tag pairs will always contain the same opening tag name as the closing tag name.

It is important to note that while most tags come in pairs, with an opening and a closing tag, sometimes tags can be just an opening tag, without the need for a closing tag. We will explore this concept later in this chapter.

Tags can also be nested within other tags; this is useful for when you want a piece of content to sit inside another piece of content. For example, you might want some text inside a box; in this case you would nest the text tag inside the tag for your box. Let's see a syntax example below:

```
<tag>
<tag2>
content
</tag2>
</tag>
```

Tags can only ever be closed directly after the opening tag. Think of it like putting a box inside another box; you need to close the inside box before closing the outside box. These tags within tags are referred to as nested elements.

When nesting elements inside other elements, it is considered best practice to indent the nested element by one tab space. This improves readability and helps us to easily see the nesting structure, and thus deduce how the tags are nested. This helps to stop documents from becoming messy and confusing. Conveniently, Sublime Text has an inbuilt tool to auto nest our tags. When we create a new tag inside another tag, Sublime Text will automatically indent the tag for us. On top of this, we are able to highlight all of the text in a document, then head over to edit > line > reindent – this will then auto-indent the entire document. Look at how much easier the text in Figure 2.1 is to read now that we have auto-indented it.

2.1

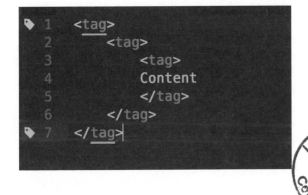

There are many different tags that can be used in our HTML document. Let's use some now by starting our first webpage build.

Creating our website template

We will start by creating the foundation for our HTML document. Follow along with the steps below to put into practice what we are learning.

Each HTML document will start with the same tags, which simply describe your webpage as a whole to the browser. Start by installing and opening up your text editor of choice and creating a new file. Call it 'index.html'. Inside this blank document, we will be constructing our very first webpage.

We'll start by declaring the document type. This snippet of code is responsible for explaining to the browser what our document is and how to display it. The tag must appear only once in a document, and must appear at the very top of the page, before any other code is written.

The syntax of the code is as follows:

```
<!DOCTYPE html>
```

Nice and simple, right? This text simply tells the browser that this is an HTML document, and to treat it as such. This line of code isn't actually an HTML tag, it is merely a declaration, an instruction to the web browser.

Once we have declared our file an HTML document, we can start writing our HTML code, so what better way to start our HTML code than with an HTML tag.

```
<html>
</html>
```

Between these tags we will nest all of our HTML code. These HTML tags simply state where the HTML code starts and where it ends. Remember HTML is simply a combination of tags and text. Let's write this HTML code now.

First, we will make use of a tag called 'head'. This tag is responsible for containing our page's metadata. In here we will specify information that is not displayed on the webpage, but is used by our browser to help explain how our webpage works.

```
<head>
</head>
```

We will be elaborating on this tag and section in future chapters, but for now, we're just going to be adding in a page title. You guessed it, using the 'title' tag. The title tag is used to give the webpage a name. This title is what will be displayed on the tab in the browser for your webpage. Let's see how it works.

```
<head>
<title>Example Webpage Title</title>
</head>
```

This small snippet of code will outline the name used for bookmarks of your webpage in a browser, the tab bar text/window header text and anywhere else where your webpage is referenced directly. Figure 2.2 is an example of how our example title will appear in Google Chrome's tab bar.

.2

After our closing 'head' tag, we will now add our 'body' tag. A body tag is responsible for declaring where the visible part of the

HTML document starts and ends. Inside our body tag, we will house our actual content. Currently, your file should look like this:

```
<!DOCTYPE html>
<html>
  <head>
    <title>Example Webpage Title</title>
  </head>
  <body>
  </body>
</html>
```

Notice how the body tag closes, then the <html> tag closes? Remember, a tag must close directly after the opening tag without any other closing tag in between.

This basic structure defines the basis of all webpages, and is what we will be working from going forward. In the next chapter we will be writing our HTML code between these body tags. This is the code that the browser will interpret and display to the end user.

Exercise

Follow the steps above so that you are left with the same code outlined at the end of the section. Save the file you created (index. html) and open it in your web browser (usually file > open in the menu). You should notice how the web browser returns a blank page. This is because tags are only ever interpreted by the web browser, never displayed. Try typing some text between the body tags – notice how the webpage displays the text you typed and nothing else. This is the principle on which websites are displayed. Learning how the browser handles tags, and understanding that these tags are merely instructions to the browser, telling it what type of content sits inside, is fundamental to your learning of HTML. By understanding this principle, you have mastered the first and most fundamentally important step in learning how to write efficient and semantic HTML code.

Table 2.2 Text glossary

Semantic	Giving meaning to information in order to allow a computer to interpret it successfully

Text

Header tags

HTML header tags are used to tell the browser where our headers are situated. They tell the browser which text is more important, and how important it is. Header tags are very simple to write; they are defined using <h1> through to <h6> tags, h1 being the most important level of header text, and h6 being the least important header text. Let's explore this further by writing some code.

In between your <body> tags, copy and paste the following text:

This is a header

This is a subheader

Save your file and open it in your browser. Notice how it all appears together in one big chunk? This is because we haven't told the browser how our content is broken up. Now copy the code below into your file and refresh your webpage.

```
<h1>This is a header</h1>
<h2>This is a subheader<h2>
```

Notice how the browser interpreted your tags and displayed your titles on separate lines and in different font sizes? This is because we have given context to our data: we have told the browser which header is more important, and which header is less important. You can use these tags any number of times across a webpage, constructing a hierarchy of data and denoting importance.

Notice how the browser knew to put each header on a new line; that's because these header elements are known as 'block elements'. You can think of a block element as an element that has an invisible box around it as wide as your webpage can go, which forces the next element to be positioned below it.

Paragraph tags

At this point you might be thinking 'what about text that isn't a header?' Well, for that we have a paragraph tag – a nice and simple little tag – denoted simply with a <p>. Contrasting with the header tag, there is only one level of paragraph tag. The <p> tag simply means paragraph. Each block of text that you would deem to be a paragraph, and so should appear as a block of text, must be contained within a <p> tag. You can have multiple <p> tags following on from one another and the browser will know to give a space between each one to denote the new paragraph. Now to put this into practice.

Let's take our code from the last section and expand on it by adding some <p> tags underneath our headers. Feel free to experiment with any number of paragraphs at any location. Take a look at this news article example:

```
<h1>Blue Peter Time Capsule Dug Up 33 years early</h1>
<p>A Blue Peter time capsule has been accidentally
dug up by construction workers 33 years earlier than
planned.</p>
<p>The Millennium Time Capsule was buried under the
Millennium Dome, now the O2 Arena, in 1998.</p>
<h2>Earlier Than anticipated<h2>
<p>A spokesperson for the BBC said: 'Although a little
earlier than anticipated, we're looking forward to
sharing these memories with our viewers and making new
ones as we return the capsule to the earth so that it
can be reopened in 2050 as originally planned.'</p>
```

Notice how we can use a mixture of header and paragraph tags to help us to give structure to our information and to outline importance and association.

Inline elements

What if we want to add some other formatting to our text inside the paragraph? Well, for that we make use of 'inline elements'. While block-level elements force stacking behaviour, by contrast, inline elements do not start new lines or disturb the flow of the document. Let's examine some inline elements, starting with a useful tag for adding an italic style to our text. For this we use the <em> tag, the 'em' meaning emphasis. We can simply wrap this tag around a word, or any number of words, to italicize the contents.

Add the <em> tag around some text in your code (making sure to close the tag at the end), save your document and refresh your webpage in your browser. Notice how your text has been italicized and is still on the same line as the other text?

There are many inline elements that we can use for styling our text, such as:

<strong> – for bold

<code> – for computer code

You might sometimes see <b> used for bold text, and <i> used for italic; these tags can be used, and are displayed in the browser in the same way. However, <strong> and <em> (meaning emphasis) are preferred as they are deemed more semantic because they describe what the content means rather than just how the text should look. For example, <bold> just means 'display text in a thicker font', whereas strong indicates 'strong importance'. It simply describes the content better.

The <br> tag

The <br> tag is a special tag – it denotes a line break. You can use the <br> tag within your paragraph tag, or your header tags; you can actually use it anywhere. It simply breaks up your content and forces whatever comes after it to appear on a new line. The <br> tag is an example of a tag that does not require a separate closing tag. It is known as an 'empty HTML element', as it has no content. While empty elements do not require a closing tag, it is considered best practice to close them in the opening tag, like so: <br/>.

Exercise

Text, and how to render it, is an extremely important and often overlooked aspect of web design. Semantically, it is hugely important to have a grasp on the best practices for marking up your text. If your page doesn't follow convention using the correct headers and paragraph tags, then search engines won't be able to interpret your content, which will result in your page not displaying correctly in search engine results pages. HTML tags give us the fantastic ability to describe our content, and take control over how we want it to look and be understood, both by humans and computers. Let's work on an example together now.

Open your webpage in your text editor and imagine you are creating a news article. You will need a headline, a few subheadlines and lots of paragraphs. You will also need some quotations. Using the tags learned in this chapter, create this news article as semantically as possible. Try to make use of all the tags we have learned. Notice how the browser displays all identical tags the same way; for example, all <h1> tags will use the same font, size and colour. Understanding this principle highlights how powerful HTML can be in helping us to create consistent-looking content without having to repeat ourselves.

Links

Links are everywhere on the web. They can take users on a journey, guiding them along the way, explaining what lies behind the new URL, or sometimes leaving it as a mystery. Links are an essential part of webpages, but how to use them well is an aspect often over-looked by many webpages. Websites are visual journeys that we take our users on. We guide them, while giving them the option of which direction to take, through the use of the links that we pro-vide. Link placement can be the difference between a successful website and a failing website. With all that responsibility on our shoulders, let's understand how to use them the right way.

What is a hyperlink?

A hyperlink is an HTML link. They allow you to navigate between various destinations on the web. A hyperlink can point to many different destinations, not just webpages. You can point your link to just about any file type imaginable.

How do we use hyperlinks?

A link tag is formatted using an <a> tag, with the following syntax:

```
<a href="exampleURL">Example link text</a>
```

The href attribute specifies the URL of the desired destination. The text between the opening and closing <a> tags is the text that will be displayed for the link. In the above example, clicking 'Example link text' would take the user to the 'exampleURL' destination.

Link formatting

There are two different ways to format your URL, using an absolute path or a relative path. Let's break down the difference in detail.

Absolute URLs

An absolute URL is a path to a resource that can exist anywhere on the web. This means it can link to a completely different website entirely. To use an absolute URL, you must format your URL with the full web address of your desired destination resource, for example 'http://www.google.com'. Clicking this URL will take the user to google.com.

Relative URLs

By contrast, a relative URL is a path to a resource that exists on the same website/server. It is a local link. Because we reference this link from your current document, we simply provide the path relative to the current document. For example, if your desired file was an HTML file that exists in the same folder as your current webpage, you would simply format your URL in the following way: 'examplefile.html'. This tells the web browser that we are looking for a file relative to the existing file. It is best practice to always use relative file paths where possible. Take the BBC website as an example. All links between the various BBC articles are relative links as they exist on the same website, and therefore the same server.

Path structures

Sometimes your destination resource resides in a different folder from your current folder. Taking the BBC as an example again, if their website was a static site, then they might have a news folder for articles, then an images folder for the images within the articles. In this case you will need to explain to the web browser how to find the file in the other folder – this can be achieved using a combination of '.' or '/'.

Let's take this document tree as an example:

www

-Webpages

--index.html

-images

--logo.png

If we wanted to provide a link from our index.html document to the logo.png file, we would use the following relative URL '../images/logo.png'. Let's break this down further: the syntax '../' denotes to the browser that you would like to traverse up the document tree, meaning to leave the current folder and move up to its parent folder. The first '..' moves up to the www folder, then the forward slash tells the browser to enter this folder. So the first '../' is saying move up to the www folder and enter it, then the second part 'images/logo.png' is requesting to enter the images folder and return the logo.png file.

This combination of '..' and '/' allows us to navigate around folder structures in order to return our relative resource.

Target attribute

When creating a hyperlink, you have the option to specify a 'target' attribute. The target attribute specifies how you want the browser to open the link. The most commonly used options for this attribute are as follows:

'_blank': this will open the resource in a new window/tab.

'_self': this will open the resource in the same window/tab. This is the default option, and will be assumed if no other target attribute is specified.

HTML bookmark

An HTML bookmark is a link that points to a specific part of a webpage. This is achieved by giving your destination an id to then point to. Let's walk through an example of how this is achieved.

First we give our desired bookmark location an id. Let's use the <h1> tag that we created earlier as an example. We simply add the following text to the opening tag <h1 id="bookmark">. Next we add our newly created id value as the href value, adding a hash at the front to denote that we are looking for a bookmark <a href="#bookmark">Link to header</a>.

Now, when the user clicks the link, the page will shift to bring the desired bookmark to the top of the page, regardless of how long the page is.

This functionality is especially useful for long webpages, where these 'jump links' can help improve the overall usability of the page.

Exercise

Now that we have learned our way around a hyperlink, let's create our first journey to send our users on. Understanding links can help to transform your website from a single webpage into a multi-page experience where the user is able to control their own journey. Adding this level of control improves the user experience as it helps your user to feel in control, which is fundamental to a good website.

Let's put what you have learned into practice. Open up your index.html file created in the previous sections. We're going to be creating an encyclopedia of your favourite images. First, save some online images you like and put them into the same folder as your index.html file. Now add some links that point to these images' locations. Now add some external links to images you have found online but haven't saved to your local disk, and be sure to open the link in a new tab so that users don't have to leave your website when they view the image. This is best practice when dealing with external links. Congratulations – you have now mastered a fundamental element of HTML. May you go forth and guide your users on many a meaningful journey.

Images

Glossary

Images are the cornerstone of modern web development: they help to provide context and meaning, they aid user engagement and they help to make web browsing a truly visual and interactive experience.

We all know how valuable images are to the overall browsing experience and, as such, it is fundamentally important to get your image selection right. In short, your image should always reflect the style and direction of your website, and most importantly, you must always ensure that you choose the correct file format for your image. Images help a website to feel alive and engaging, so let's take a look at how you can brighten up your website with some images.

Image types

There are three main image types used across the web: JPEG, PNG and GIF images. Each image type has its own benefits and uses and the image type used should be defined by the demands of the webpage.

Table 2.3   Image glossary

Lossy compression	A compression technique that improves the size of the file, but at a detriment to the image quality. Saving the same JPEG image over and over will result in lower quality each time it is saved, but also a smaller file size each time
Alpha channel	An alpha channel allows an image to utilize transparency at various points in the image
Lossless compression	A compression technique that improves the size of the file, without detriment to the image quality
Vector file format	A vector file is a graphical file that uses shapes to represent images; they are represented using points, which are numerical values, and as such they can be scaled to an infinitely large size, without any loss in quality
Raster file format	An image file format that uses a collection of pixels to represent images; their quality degrades upon an increase in file size
Screen reader	Software that allows visually impaired users to read the text that is displayed on screen, through use of a speech synthesizer or braille text

JPEG

JPEG files are mainly used for photographs as they can be highly compressed and produce very small file sizes. It is worth noting that JPEG files are a lossy file format, and as such JPEGs are not very good for logos as they can look fuzzy and they also lack an alpha channel, which restricts the ability to use transparency in the image.

GIF

GIF files are mainly used for logos and animations. GIFs offer small file sizes, and animation functionality. They are a lossless format and also allow transparency; however, GIFs are limited to just 256 colours, so are unable to produce the full spectrum of colours often required for a photograph, therefore they are typically used for simple line drawings with few colours, such as logos.

PNG (PNG-24)

PNG files are the newest file type of the bunch, and offer similar functionality to GIFs, but improve on them in almost every way. PNGs are lossless, offer better transparency support and contain a wider range of colours; however, they don't support animations and the file size is larger than JPEG and GIF. PNGs can be very useful for icons and photographs that use transparency, but the large file size means that whether to use them should be carefully considered.

SVG

SVG files are growing in popularity due to their small file size and infinite scalability. SVG files are a vector file format, compared to the above three, which are all raster file formats. This comes with many benefits, the main ones being the infinite scalability and tiny file size. These benefits make SVG perfect for icons, logos and simple graphics. Because SVGs are written using code, we can actually alter the image directly on our website, without needing to even open a photo editor.

File sizes

When working with images on your website, it's important to actively monitor the impact each image you add has on your page load speed. If the page is taking too long to load, consider either removing the image, or making it smaller. You could also make use of an online image compressor to get the file size down as much as possible. The art of balancing page load times with media-rich websites is a constant challenge for a web developer, but one that a lot of developers thrive off and find that it makes the job that bit more rewarding when you hit that sweet spot.

Syntax of an image tag

To use an image on a website, we make use of the <img> tag. The syntax is as follows:

```
<img src="image.png" alt="image description">
```

The <img> tag is an empty tag, and as such does not require a closing tag. It uses the src attribute to specify the location of the desired image and, as with the link tag, you can use either relative or absolute paths here. It's important to note that you must include the file extension at the end of the path.

The alt attribute is where we specify our alternative image text. This is used when the browser is unable to render the image (because of a slow connection, an error finding the image file or if the user is using a screen reader). It is also used to explain to search engines what your image is, so that it can then use the image in its search results.

Image size

By default an image will be loaded in its native dimensions.

> Native dimensions are the size of the image that was defined when the image was created.

However, we can override this by specifying our own dimensions, like so:

```
<img src="image.png" alt="image description" width="100"
height="70">
```

The width and height attributes are used to tell the browser what size we would like to display the image. The values used are in pixel format. It is important to note that specifying both width and height attributes will force the image into the specified aspect ratio. Therefore, if the image ratio is different from the original image, the image may look squashed or bloated. So it is common to just specify either width or height alone, which sets the size of the specified dimension and leaves the other to automatically scale as per the image's natural aspect ratio. For example, specifying a width of 100 pixels would allow the height of the image to automatically scale to the correct height to honour the image's aspect ratio.

Exercise

Enter the following URL into your browser **http://indigomelody.com/ confident-web-design/files** to download a zip file containing some example images to use on your website. Extract the folder and place it in the same directory as your index.html file, then add all five raster images to your webpage. Decide on an order for the images and ensure that you populate the alt text attribute. Then alter the widths of the images to try to get all five to render on the same line. If you are feeling curious, why not see what happens when you move one of the images outside of the images' directory. Notice how the browser handles your alt text attribute. This is what a screen reader would see.

Tables

Tables were once the main layout element of the web. They were truly on every single webpage. Before we had better styling controls with CSS, we would position everything inside one big table and break up the content into the various cells and columns. Fortunately this awkward method of laying out a website is no longer necessary, though this doesn't mean that tables have lost their place entirely on the web. They are still the preferred method of displaying structured data, and can be extremely useful for this purpose. Let's check out how to create one ourselves.

Table mark-up

A table consists of headers, rows and columns. Each row should have a header (even if it is blank), and each row should have the same number of columns as there are headers defined.

Now let's break down how we build a simple table. Tables are defined and contained within a <table> tag. Then within the opening and closing tags of the table, we can start to specify our rows. Our first row is going to be our header row, so we must create a new row using the <tr> tag, like so:

```
<table>
  <tr>
  </tr>
</table>
```

Now we have a new row within our table, so let's add some column headers to this row using the <th> tag. Within the opening and closing <th> tags, we specify our header text. There's no limit to how many columns we can add, but in our example we are only going to add three.

```
<table>
  <tr>
    <th>Firstname</th>
    <th>Lastname</th>
    <th>Date of Birth</th>
  </tr>
</table>
```

By default the header row is styled with bold and centred text to help add emphasis. Now that we have finished the header row, we can move on to our data rows, so we now simply add a new row (<tr>) directly below the closing tag of our previous row.

```
<table>
  <tr>
    <th>Firstname</th>
    <th>Lastname</th>
    <th>Date of Birth</th>
  </tr>
  <tr>
  </tr>
</table>
```

Within this row, we are going to be adding our data. Because we are now adding a data cell instead of a heading, we are going to be using the <td> tag. Similarly to the table heading tags, our information goes between the opening and closing tags. We can add any content we like inside this cell, including another table. Remember, we must ensure that we have an equal number of cells to that of our header row. So let's add three again.

```html
<table>
  <tr>
    <th>Firstname</th>
    <th>Lastname</th>
    <th>Date of Birth</th>
  </tr>
  <tr>
    <td>Joe</td>
    <td>Bloggs</td>
    <td>12/01/1970</td>
  </tr>
</table>
```

If we want to add more rows of data, we simply repeat this process of adding rows below rows until we have added all of the necessary information.

```html
<table>
  <tr>
    <th>Firstname</th>
    <th>Lastname</th>
    <th>Date of Birth</th>
  </tr>
  <tr>
    <td>Joe</td>
    <td>Bloggs</td>
    <td>12/01/1970</td>
  </tr>
  <tr>
    <td>Jane</td>
    <td>Bloggs</td>
    <td>12/02/1972</td>
  </tr>
</table>
```

Exercise

Follow the steps above to create the same table structure in your index.html file. Then experiment with adding a new table within your created table. This method of nesting tables within other tables is the principle on which HTML emails are written. Whenever you see a pretty email reach your inbox, what you are effectively seeing is a bunch of columns and rows nested within each other to create what typically appears to be a seamless image. The reason we build emails using tables is because email clients tend to use old versions of popular internet browsers to render their emails, and often don't support more modern features, which forces us to use tables, as they have been supported from the early foundations of the internet. This challenge is reminiscent of many other challenges a web developer faces when building a website. Compatibility among the array of devices available is a constantly evolving challenge that keeps web developers on their toes and forces them to keep up to date with the latest technological advances.

Lists

Who doesn't love a good old list? Lists are actually used a lot in web design. Surprisingly, the majority of navigation bars you see are actually created as lists in HTML. Their uses extend much further than that, though. We often also use lists for image slideshows among other things, not to mention, whenever we want to create, you know, a list. There are a few different types of list we can create depending upon our needs. Let's check them out below.

List types

The three types of lists that are available to us are as follows:

- Unordered list: a collection of items without any specific ordering, with each new list item marked with a bullet point (by default, but can be changed later on).

- Ordered list: a collection of items that do appear in a specific order or sequence, with each new list item being marked with an auto-incrementing number.

- Definition list: a list where each list item consists of a term followed by a definition.

Unordered lists

Unordered lists are initiated with the <ul> element, with the opening and closing tags wrapping around our list in its entirety. Each 'list item' is then initiated with the <li> element, wrapping the opening (<li>) and closing (</li>) tags around the list item's text, as can be seen below:

```
<ul>
  <li>List Item 1</li>
  <li>List Item 2</li>
  <li>List Item 3</li>
  <li>List Item 4</li>
  <li>List Item 5</li>
</ul>
```

You will notice how we don't specify that we would like a bullet point, yet in the browser each list item still has a bullet point prefixing it by default. We will explore some of the possibilities of this behaviour later in this book.

Ordered lists

Ordered lists are structurally identical to unordered lists, however instead of using a <ul> tag to wrap around our list items, we replace it with an <ol> tag instead. Everything else can stay the same.

```
<ol>
  <li>List Item 1</li>
  <li>List Item 2</li>
  <li>List Item 3</li>
  <li>List Item 4</li>
  <li>List Item 5</li>
</ol>
```

Notice how, once again, we don't specify the numbering for each list item, but our browser displays the numbers by default.

OL attributes

Type attribute

We can modify how our numbering scheme is displayed by using the type attribute on the opening <ol> tag. We can use the following values to alter the appearance of the numbers:

type="1" – list items will be ordered with numbers (this is the default behaviour).

type="A" – list items will be ordered with uppercase letters.

type="a" – list items will be ordered with lowercase letters.

type="I" – list items will be ordered with uppercase roman numerals.

type="i" – list items will be ordered with lowercase roman numerals.

Start attribute

We can also modify the number from which you would like the ordering to start from by using the 'start' attribute as seen below.

```
<ol start="7">
```

In the above example the list would begin at 7, then continue to 8, and so on. Likewise, if we were creating an alphabetical list, it would start from the seventh letter of the alphabet, so in this case the list would start at 'G' and continue on to H and onwards.

Description lists

Description lists, also referred to as 'definition lists' in older versions of HTML, are used to list terms alongside their definitions. A definition list is made up of three tags: the surrounding <dl> tag which defines your description list; a <dt> tag for the term/name; and lastly a <dd> tag for the definition. The structure of the list is very similar to the previous two lists, but for a definition list we simply write the <dt> tag (term) first, followed by the <dd> tag (definition) and then move on to the next <dt> tag and <dd> tag pairs. As we can see below:

```
<dl>
   <dt>Term 1</dt>
   <dd>Definition 1</dd>
   <dt>Term 2</dt>
   <dd>Definition 2</dd>
   <dt>Term 3</dt>
   <dd>Definition 3</dd>
</dl>
```

When this list is viewed in a browser the definition will be displayed below its parent term and indented one tab space from the left. It is important to note that you are not limited to just one definition per term, you are able to specify multiple definitions by simply adding another <dd> element below your existing <dd> element for the parent term, as is seen below:

```
<dl>
   <dt>Term 1</dt>
   <dd>Definition 1</dd>
   <dd>Definition 1 - 2</dd>
```

```
    <dt>Term 2</dt>
    <dd>Definition 2</dd>
    <dt>Term 3</dt>
    <dd>Definition 3</dd>
  </dl>
```

Displaying lists

At this point you might have noticed that when a list is rendered in the browser, it always renders on a new line and without any other content next to it. This happens regardless of how much horizontal space the list takes up. This is because all list types are block-level elements. (Remember, block-level elements will always start on a new line by default.)

Exercise

As we already know, lists are often used in web design for purposes that you might not expect, such as in navigation sections, which are actually lists of links formatted to be displayed horizontally. Lists are also used for image slideshows. Following the steps above and using what we have learned so far in the previous sections, create an image list comprising of some of our gallery images.

What we have learned in this chapter

This chapter has introduced HTML – an essential language for every web developer. The next chapter will complete the section on HTML by covering the final basic concepts – forms, divs and spans, and element identifiers – and will guide you in bringing all these together and creating your very first webpage.

03
HTML Part 2

What we will learn in this chapter

This chapter will conclude the section on HTML by covering forms, divs and spans, and element identifiers. This will then show you how to construct a website structure using HTML.

Forms

Forms are everywhere on the web, from 'contact us', to payment information forms and signing up to mailing lists, they are a fundamental part of web design. Forms allow your users to reach out and make contact with you, which is typically one of the key goals of any website: user engagement. Forms are useful for gathering information from your users. A common goal of a form is obtain your users' email address so that you can target them with email alerts about your website. Forms are a fantastic way to encourage communication from your users, whether it be for collecting feedback or simply offering users the opportunity to 'get in touch' with enquiries, there are few better options for adding a communication method to your website than through a web form, and they are actually fairly easy to set up. First, let's take a closer look at how they work.

How forms work

Forms can be separated into two parts. The first is the form itself, which contains the fields, buttons, dropdowns, text boxes and radio buttons. The second is the part that contains the logic, or the script, which will take the information submitted, perform an action on it and return a result. This script is usually carried out on the server and, as such, is written using a server-side scripting language such as PHP. For the purpose of this book, we will be performing our form action right in the browser.

Creating a form

Forms are created using the <form> element, which wraps around our form content, which will be made up of, but not limited to, buttons and input fields. We can also include other elements, such as heading tags and paragraphs inside our <form> tag without any issues. It is important to note that you cannot nest a form inside another form as this will break the form's functionality.

The two most common attributes that are used on the <form> element are the method and action attributes. Let's break down what these are responsible for...

Form action

The action element is where we tell the browser what we want the form to do when submitted by the end user. The value should provide the location of the script that is to be run on submit. Typically you might see a value in here like so:

```
<form action="/scripts/contactForm.php">
```

When the form is submitted, the script found on the server at the specified address (/scripts/contactForm.php) will be run. As with all URLs this can be either a relative or an absolute path.

The action doesn't always have to be a script, however. You can also provide other actions, for example opening a link to a new page. In our example we are going to be using the form to open up a new draft email with the to: field already populated. For this we are going to be using the following form action:

```
<form action="mailto:someone@example.com?subject=
Example %20Subject">
```

mailto: functions as a link to open up a new draft message in the user's default email client. The value directly after the mailto: syntax is the destination email address; the text after '?subject=' will be the subject line of the draft email. The text '%20' in the subject action will render as a space. We use this code as spaces are not allowed in the query string.

Form method

When creating a form, the method attribute should be completed along with the action attribute. The method simply states how the information in the form should be transferred to the action attribute's destination address. This can be in one of two ways: GET or POST.

GET method

The GET method, which is the form's default method, is a way of sending the information via the URL. The information from the form will be appended to the URL, which will then be interpreted by the script at the action attribute's value. An example of this might be as follows: contactUs.php?firstname=Joe&lastname=Bloggs

In the above example, the script contactUs.php will be passed by two variables.

Variable: a keyword identifier that contains a value.

Firstname, which has the value Joe, and lastname, which has the value Bloggs. The script will then perform an action using these variables, and return a result.

POST method

The POST method is used when you want to hide information from the URL. This is especially useful when dealing with sensitive data, such as passwords and credit card details.

<input>

A form is nothing without some inputs for us to enter our information into. There are no shortage of input types at our disposal, but for now we will look at one basic example and break down how it functions within the form. For this we will take a look at a text input field. A text input field is created as follows:

```
<input type="text" name="firstname">
```

Notice how we use the <input> element to denote that we want an input on the form, then the type of input we are requesting is defined in the type attribute. This is the same for all the various input types.

Also notice the name attribute. This attribute is essential and required for your input to be submitted by the form. It is fundamentally important that you always include the name attribute on all of your inputs that are to be submitted.

The above code will generate a blank input field for your user to enter their information into. However, there's currently no label explaining what information is required. For this we can make use of the <label> tag.

Though not required, it's important for optimal usability to ensure your input fields are labelled for your user. The <label> element can be used in conjunction with your inputs to provide some context and meaning around your input fields. See the below example:

```
<label for="firstname">First Name</label>
<input type="text" id="firstname" name="first name"/>
```

In the above example we can see that we add a 'for' attribute, which will contain the ID of the input field it is associated with. You will notice we have also added an ID attribute to the input tag matching this label's 'for' attribute. Inside the opening and closing tags we can specify our label, which will be visible in the browser. This label text can be anything at all without any restrictions.

The inputs

As you already know, forms are made up of a number of different inputs ranging from text input fields, to passwords, sliders and dropdowns. It is important that a web developer understands the full extent of the input options available to them. Table 3.1 outlines the various inputs along with a brief explanation and example mark-up.

Table 3.1   Input types

Input type	Definition	Example
Text	Defines a one-line text input field	`<input type="text" id="firstname" name ="firstname">`
Password	Defines a password field with the inputted text converted into asterisks	`<input type="password" name="psw">`
Submit	Defines a button which, when clicked, will submit the form data to the 'form-handler' (the value of action attribute)	`<input type="submit" value="Submit">`
Reset	Defines a button which, when clicked, will clear all the inputted data and revert them back to their original default values	`<input type="reset">`

(continued)

Table 3.1 (Continued)

Input type	Definition	Example
Radio	Defines a set of radio buttons, which will restrict the user to only selecting one of the options presented	`<input type="radio" name="gender" value="male" checked> Male `
		`<input type="radio" name="gender" value="female"> Female `
		`<input type="radio" name="gender" value="other"> Other`
Checkbox	Defines a set of checkboxes, which will allow the user to select multiple options, including selecting none at all	`<input type="checkbox" name="vehicle1" value="Bike"> I have a bike `
		`<input type="checkbox" name="vehicle2" value="Car"> I have a car`
Button	Defines a button for use with JavaScript (more on this later)	`<input type="button" onclick="alert('Hello World!')" value="Click Me!">`

Other input types

There are a small number of elements that break the mould of the standard input types and instead of utilizing the type attribute of the <input> element, they exist as stand-alone elements that operate in very much the same way as the <input> tag. They are as follows:

\<textarea\>

The \<textarea\> element is the only input type that breaks from the above standard of defining the input type in the type attribute. The \<textarea\> element is a stand-alone element and can be defined as follows:

```
<textarea name="message" rows="10">
The cat was playing in the garden.
</textarea>
```

The above example will generate a multi-line input field with 10 lines available for our users to input text into.

\<select\>

The \<select\> element is another element that does not utilize the type attribute of the input field for its generation. Instead, the \<select\> element operates similarly to the text area element. The \<select\> element is responsible for creating a dropdown box for the user to select. The syntax for a select box is as follows:

```
<select name="cars">
    <option value="volvo">Volvo</option>
    <option value="saab">Saab</option>
    <option value="fiat">Fiat</option>
    <option value="audi">Audi</option>
</select>
```

Notice how it still has the name attribute even though it is not an input tag. For the \<select\> element, the option tags are used to specify the values that can be selected from the dropdown. The value attribute is the key for the option that will be passed on to the form action. The text between the opening and closing option tags is what the user will see. You are able to have different keys from the labels of the options. For example, it is not uncommon for a select box to be marked up as follows:

```
<select name="cars">
    <option value="1">Volvo</option>
    <option value="2">Saab</option>
    <option value="3">Fiat</option>
    <option value="4">Audi</option>
</select>
```

In this example, if the user selects Saab as their option and submits the form using the submit button, the form action will be passed the value of 2 for the 'cars' variable.

Grouping data

Forms can easily get messy and confusing, so it's important that we maintain a high level of usability throughout when we are building them. Fortunately we can make use of two very important elements to help with this. They are the <fieldset> element, and the <legend> element.

Let's see how they work.

<fieldset>

As you probably guessed, a <fieldset> element is what we will use to group together a group of fields of related data into a set. For example, we might have a fieldset for all of the address fields of a contact form, or we might have one for personal information in a sign-up form. Fieldsets can drastically help to improve the user experience of your form. The syntax is nice and simple too. As you've also probably guessed by now, you simply wrap your <fieldset> tags around your related fields and that's it. See below for an example:

```
<fieldset>
   First name:<br>
   <input type="text" id="firstname" name="firstname"
      value="Mickey"><br>
   Last name:<br>
   <input type="text" name="lastname"
      value="Mouse"><br><br>
   <input type="submit" value="Submit">
</fieldset>
```

<legend>

Now that we have a fieldset, it's important to label these fields to provide context and meaning to your users around the grouped fields. For this we can use the <legend> element to add a caption/label to the fieldset.

We can use the <legend> element by simply wrapping our text inside the <legend> tags. Ensure this element is the first element inside the fieldset, and it will display nicely in the browser and add to the overall user experience of your form. See below for an example of the element in action:

```
<fieldset>
   <legend>Personal information:</legend>
   First name:<br>
   <input type="text" id="firstname" name="firstname"
      value="Mickey"><br>
   Last name:<br>
   <input type="text" name="lastname"
      value="Mouse"><br><br>
   <input type="submit" value="Submit">
</fieldset>
```

Putting it all together

We have now seen the individual aspects of the web form. Let's now put it all back together and see an example form in action. We will use a simple example of a form with two text input fields, a submit button and a reset button. Note that all the inputs have the name attribute completed. Without these attributes completed, the values wouldn't be passed through to the email body.

```
<form action="mailto:someone@example.com" method=
   "post">
   Name:<br>
   <input type="text" name="name"><br>
   E-mail:<br>
   <input type="text" name="mail"><br>
   <input type="submit" value="Send">
   <input type="reset" value="Reset">
</form>
```

Exercise

Now that we are familiar with the various elements that make up a form, it is time for you to try to put one together yourself. Open up your index.html file and copy the above example into it. Now you can experiment around with the various different input types available to us, and explore what happens when you submit the form. How are the values displayed in the draft email? Try removing a name attribute from one of the fields. How does it affect things? Why not try expanding upon the example given above and introduce field sets and legends to improve its usability?

Divs and spans

Div

A div is a block-level element that acts a bit like a container. It is used to group together content on our webpage. It is most useful as a method of grouping content into an easily targetable element. The <div> element has no required attributes; however, both id and class attributes are often used in conjunction with divs as a method of giving the content a name that canbe used for styling the group. The syntax for using a <div> element is nice and simple. We simply wrap our <div> opening and closing tags around the content we want to group logically. For example, we might have an <h1> tag followed by a series of paragraphs about the headline, relating to a topic like so:

```
<h1>Business Name </h1>
<p>Business Slogan.</p>
<p>Paragraph about your business</p>
```

It would be logical to group these elements together using a div so that we can easily target this specific block. An example of this would be:

```
<div>
   <h1>John Doe </h1>
   <p>Paragraph about John Doe.</p>
   <p>Another paragraph about John Doe</p>
</div>
```

You can also nest divs inside other divs; for example, we might want to group together a group of divs relating to content about people. An example of this might be:

```
<div>
   <div>
      <h1>John Doe </h1>
      <p>Paragraph about John Doe.</p>
      <p>Another paragraph about John Doe</p>
   </div>
   <div>
      <h1>Jane Doe </h1>
      <p>Paragraph about Jane Doe.</p>
      <p>Another paragraph about Jane Doe</p>
   </div>
</div>
```

By grouping these elements together, we can then easily target all of the topics, or each individual topic. This allows us to be as generic or granular with our targeting as possible.

Span

Span elements are largely identical to divs; however, where divs are block-level elements, span elements are inline elements. This means that span tags can be used on text, where divs cannot. An example of this might be as follows:

```
<p>Some <span>example</span> text</p>
```

As you can see, this span allows us to target an individual word in a sentence. This span element can then be directly targeted and used to style that individual word as necessary.

> ## Exercise
>
> Taking what we have learned in this chapter, open up your index.
> html page and have a look through what you have written so far.
> Let's group together the code from each section into separate
> divs. Wrap your div tags around the elements you have created so
> far into logical groupings based on the section title (forms,
> images, etc). Grouping together related content is key to keeping
> your website content organized and easily targeted. Experiment
> with adding more divs and spans within your new divs around
> individual elements.

Element identifiers

To mark the end of this section's coverage of concepts, we find
ourselves looking at element identifiers; this is where web design
really comes alive. Element identifiers are how we target elements
on our page. They help us to define areas of our page, which in turn
allows us to target and style those areas as per our requirements.
What you are about to learn is one of the most useful features of
HTML and opens up the doors to more exciting possibilities when
styling and targeting content.

The id identifier

We use an id identifier to define a unique element in our webpage.
Ids are placed on elements where the content is purely unique and
only used once across the webpage. For example, a logo would
typically be given an id, as there is only one logo on a page, and it
is a unique piece of content. Another example might be if you were
to have a webpage with a list of products. Each product is unique
and therefore could have a unique id relating to its product number to allow us to locate each product easily. Ids are attributes, and

as such we assign them in the exact same way we have assigned all of our attributes in the previous chapters, inside the opening tag.

Because ids' names tend to be quite descriptive in nature – to help us remember exactly what content we are defining – it is common to name ids with a phrase. For example we might want to identify a sidebar that sits on the left of the page by calling it 'left sidebar', however, id names cannot have any spaces in them, so as a best practice in web development, we tend to hyphenate the word, replacing the spaces hyphens. Therefore, in our example 'left sidebar', our identifier would become 'left-sidebar'. Let's see this in action:

```
<div id="left-sidebar">
    <ul>
        <li>Sidebar item 1</li>
        <li>Sidebar item 2</li>
        <li>Sidebar item 3</li>
    </ul>
</div>
```

Remember, you can always nest divs inside one another, so you can also nest ids. On top of this, you can apply ids to the majority of elements in HTML, not just divs. Let's see an example of nested ids and ids on elements other than divs:

```
<div id="left-sidebar">
    <ul>
        <li id="sidebar-item1">Sidebar item 1</li>
        <li id="sidebar-item2">Sidebar item 2</li>
        <li id="sidebar-item3">Sidebar item 3</li>
    </ul>
</div>
```

The class identifier

The class identifier, like the id identifier, is used for naming our content; however, where ids are used for unique pieces of content, classes are used for elements of a similar nature. They are used as a way to ensure consistency between these elements. By labelling similar elements with the same class, we are able to select multiple elements at the same time. Let's continue our above example of the left sidebar. Let's assume that we want our three sidebar items to look identical, just with different content; we might want to give our items a class to share so that we can target the three items at the same time. This becomes very powerful when styling the divs as we don't have to repeat the styling process for each div individually (more on styling in the next chapter). Just like the id identifier, it is an attribute, and is assigned as such. Let's see our sidebar item example again, but this time using classes.

```
<div id="left-sidebar">
    <ul>
        <li class="sidebar-item">Sidebar item 1</li>
        <li class="sidebar-item">Sidebar item 2</li>
        <li class="sidebar-item">Sidebar item 3</li>
    </ul>
</div>
```

As you can see, the three items all share the exact same class, despite having different content. This is absolutely fine, as the class simply states that the content is of the same type, not that it is identical. You might also notice that we have nested our classes inside a main div with an id. This is absolutely fine too – we can nest ids inside classes and vice versa without any issues.

Not only can we nest ids and classes within one another, we can also apply an id and classes to the same item. Let's see this in action...

```
<div id="left-sidebar">
  <ul>
    <li id="sidebar-item1" class="sidebarItem">Sidebar
      item 1</li>
    <li id="sidebar-item2" class="sidebarItem">Sidebar
      item 2</li>
    <li id="sidebar-item3" class="sidebarItem">Sidebar
      item 3</li>
  </ul>
</div>
```

This is a very powerful technique as it allows us to now target all of the items at once using the class 'sidebar-item', or on an individual level using their unique id.

One last important concept to understand about classes is that we can apply multiple classes to the same element. This allows us to assign elements to multiple different 'groups' that we can target. For example, we might want to be able to select the first item of every list across the whole website, so that we can increase its font size. For this we would assign the same class to the first item of each list, which would allow us to target every first list element at the same time. Continuing our example, let's see how this looks:

```
<div id="left-sidebar">
  <ul>
    <li id="left-sidebar-item1" class="sidebar-item
      first-list-item">Sidebar item 1
    </li>
    <li id="left-sidebar-item2" class="sidebar-
      item">Sidebar item 2</li>
    <li id="left-sidebar-item3" class="sidebar-
      item">Sidebar item 3</li>
  </ul>
</div>
```

```
<div id="right-sidebar">
 <ul>
  <li id="right-sidebar-Item1" class="sidebar-item
     first-listitem">Sidebar item 1</li>
  <li id="right-sidebar-Item2" class="sidebar-item
     first-listitem">Sidebar item 2</li>
  <li id="right-sidebar-Item3" class="sidebar-item
     first-listitem">Sidebar item 3</li>
  </ul>
</div>
```

As you can see from our above example, we have given the same 'first-list-item' class to the first list-items in each of our sidebar lists. We can now use the 'first-list-item' class to target all of the first list-items on our webpage, or we can use the 'sidebarItem' class to target all of our list-items. Alternatively we could use any of their ids to target them on an individual level. This is a very powerful function of ids and classes, which allows us complete flexibility in how granular or general we want to be in our targeting. You will also notice how the classes are separated by a single space. This is important: never use commas, semi-colons or any other delimiters here. A simple space is enough to separate our classes.

Exercise

Open up your index.html document and work through your content applying ids and classes to your divs where you see fit. Then move on to your other elements and continue to apply ids and classes where appropriate. Remember you can apply ids and classes to inline elements as well as block-level elements.

Putting it all together: creating your first website

Part 1 has seen us learn the core elements of the HTML language. We got to grips with the syntax of HTML and how we structure our content. We tackled text, images, links and lists. We saw the use and power of a web form before creating our own version. We now understand how divs help us to break up our content and how powerful giving divs an id and/or class can be. At this stage, you have learned enough to structure a full website complete with all the typical elements we see across the web today. You have understood the use of hyphens in class names and understood the importance of setting logical ids and classnames. This principle extends further than just HTML into other programming languages. You are now well on your way to creating your first fully functional website, and becoming a certified web developer.

We have learned a lot in this section, so let's now consolidate what we know and use it to start to build our actual website. You can use the index.html document that you have created so far as a reference along with this book to help you through the exercises.

We will now run through each of the topics we have covered in this section and outline an exercise to be completed on that topic. You should download the source files from **http://indigomelody.com/ABCDEFG** to use in the exercises. Now is your chance to put everything we have learned into practice and create your first full HTML webpage. By the end of this you will have created the first of the three parts of your first fully functional website, as such.

> It is important to ensure that you complete these tasks, as the webpages you create here in this section will be used in subsequent sections of the book.

Template

We will begin by recapping what we learned in the basics section of this chapter. We started by constructing the base structure a webpage takes before we add in our actual content. The great thing about this template is that this base structure will be the same on all pages regardless of what content we add, so we only need to create this once and copy it across to any subsequent pages we write.

Exercise

1 In the root folder, create a new file called index.html and open it in our text editor.

2 Create our base structure using the doctype, html, head, title and body tags.

3 Enter the title 'Web Design Components'.

Introduction text

In Chapter 2, we discussed how to use the various text-related tags to create hierarchy and importance among your content. We introduced the <h> and <p> tags and their variants. In Chapter 3 we discussed divs and highlighted their use in grouping content together. Then finally we introduced ids and classes and how they are used to identify content and use those identifiers to target our content. Let's put these tags to use now by giving our webpage an introductory section of text and wrapping it in a div.

Exercise

1 Inside the <body> tags, write the following snippet of text as header text 'Webpage components'.

2 Enter the following text as paragraph text: 'This website contains all of the basic elements used to create a webpage.'

> **3** Wrap these snippets of text in a div and give it an id of 'introduction-text'.
>
> **4** Wrap a <span> tag around the first word of the paragraph and give it a class of 'firstWord'.

Images

In Chapter 2, we demonstrated how to make use of images in web design and how to set fixed heights to our images. Let's now add some images into our website.

> ### **Exercise**
>
> **1** Above our 'introduction-text' div, add a new div with a class of 'full-width-image'.
>
> **2** Inside this div add the 'introduction.jpg' image from the images folder.
>
> **3** Give the image an alt value of 'Introduction header image'.

Tables

In Chapter 2, we highlighted the use of tables in web design and detailed how to use them. We explored the importance of ensuring the column count is consistent among rows and explored the default styling of the header row. Let's create an example table for our reference now:

> ### **Exercise**
>
> **1** Create a new div with the id 'tables' and the class of 'new-section'.
>
> **2** Inside this div create a new div with the class of 'section-header'.

3 Inside the 'section-header' div create a header with the title 'Tables'.

4 Then below the 'section-header' div create a new div with the class 'section-body'.

5 Inside the 'section-body' div create a table with three columns.

6 In the top header row, enter the following column headers from left to right: 'id', 'First Name', 'Email'.

7 Then in the body, enter as many rows as you would like and enter some dummy information.

Lists

In Chapter 2, we broke down the difference between the various lists that are available to us. We explored some examples of when an ordered list is more useful than an unordered list and also outlined the use of a definition list. Let's document this in our website for future reference.

Exercise

1 Create a copy of the div with the 'tables' id, including all the nested content.

2 Paste this below the 'tables' div.

3 Now replace the 'tables' id with 'lists' and also replace the header text from 'section-header' to say 'Lists'.

4 Remove all nested divs from the 'section-body' div.

5 Then, inside the 'section-body', create the following, each below the previous:

– An <h2> tag with the text 'Unordered List Example'.

– An unordered list containing three list items called 'Unordered List Item 1' with the number ascending with each new list item.

– An <h2> tag with the text 'Ordered List Example'.

- An ordered list containing three list items called 'Ordered List Item 1' with the number ascending with each new list item.
- An <h2> tag with the text 'Definition List Example'.
- A definition list containing three list terms called 'Definition List Term 1' with the number ascending with each new list item, followed by their corresponding definition examples.

Forms

Chapter 3 saw us explore the use of forms in web design. We understood how they function and also how they are created. We then broke down the main components that are used to construct a form and saw the differences between them and how they operate within the form. We also introduced the functionality of opening a draft email in the user's email client, which we put into practice for our form action. Let's replicate this on our website for future reference.

Exercise

1 Once again, start by creating a copy of the div with the 'tables' id, including all the nested content.

2 Paste this below the 'lists' div.

3 Now replace the 'tables' id with 'forms' and also replace the header text from 'section-header' to say 'Forms'.

4 Remove all nested divs from the 'section-body' div.

5 Then, inside the 'section-body', create a new form.

6 Inside the form tags, create three input fields: one for first name, one for surname, and finally one for email address, ensuring that you use the correct input types for each.

7 Break up each input with a line break to force each input onto a row on its own.

8 Create labels for each input and then finish it off with a submit button.

9 Give the form an action of a mailto with the to: address set to 'contact@website.com' and a subject of 'New User Request'.

Links

We focused on links in Chapter 2 and worked through the different ways we can instruct the browser to open the link using the 'target' attribute. We introduced the concept of absolute and relative urls and when to use one over the other. We also saw path structures and learned how to use a path structure to navigate through directories. We lastly saw bookmarks and how to scroll the webpage to a specific section in the website. Let's now pull together what we have learned about links, and more specifically HTML bookmarking, to create a navigational structure to finish off our website.

Exercise

1 Start at the very top of the <body> element. Just after the opening <body> tag, create a new unordered list.

2 Create list items for each of the sections we created in the above exercises with the class 'new-section'.

3 Then within each list item, create a link to the corresponding div id.

4 Use the heading from each div as the link text.

5 You should end up with a 'jump list', which will take you to each of the sections on your webpage. Finally, wrap a div with the id 'jump-list' around your list and that will bring this chapter to a close.

What we have learned in the HTML section: final code output

If you followed Part 1 exactly, you should end up with a webpage identical to the below code. Well done! You have just created a full webpage using a wide variety of the most vital HTML elements. We will be using this webpage for the subsequent sections, where we will be styling the HTML output that we have written, using CSS. This is where you can start to unleash your creative side as we make our website more visually pleasing and start to give our website a style. If you have not been able to complete all of the exercises, or if your code is different from the expected output below, it is vitally important that you alter your code to be identical to the below output.

```
INDEX.HTML
<!DOCTYPE html>
<html>
    <head>
        <title>Web Design Components</title>
    </head>
    <body>
        <div id="jump-list">
            <ul>
                <li><a href="#tables">Tables</a></li>
                <li><a href="#lists">Lists</a></li>
                <li><a href="#forms">Forms</a></li>
            </ul>
        </div>
        <div class="full-width-image">
            <img src="images/introduction.jpg"
                alt="Introduction header image">
        </div>
```

```html
<div id="introduction-text">
   <h1>Webpage components</h1>
   <p><span class="first-word">This</span>
      website contains all of the basic elements
      used to create a webpage</p>
</div>
<div id="tables" class="new-section">
   <div class="section-header">
      <h1>Tables</h1>
   </div>
   <div class="section-body">
      <table>
         <tr>
            <th>id</th>
            <th>First Name</th>
            <th>email</th>
         </tr>
         <tr>
            <td>1</td>
            <td>John</td>
            <td>john@email.com</td>
         </tr>
         <tr>
            <td>2</td>
            <td>Jane</td>
            <td>jane@email.com</td>
         </tr>
      </table>
   </div>
</div>
<div id="lists" class="new-section">
   <div class="section-header">
      <h1>Lists</h1>
```

```
        </div>
        <div class="section-body">
            <h2>Unordered List Example</h2>
            <ul>
                <li>Ordered List Item 1</li>
                <li>Ordered List Item 2</li>
                <li>Ordered List Item 3</li>
            </ul>
            <h2>Ordered List Example</h2>
            <ol>
                <li>Ordered List Item 1</li>
                <li>Ordered List Item 2</li>
                <li>Ordered List Item 3</li>
            </ol>
            <h2>Definition List Example</h2>
            <dl>
                <dt>Definition List Term 1</dt>
                <dd>Definition List Definition 1</dd>
                <dt>Definition List Term 2</dt>
                <dd>Definition List Definition 2</dd>
                <dt>Definition List Term 3</dt>
                <dd>Definition List Definition 3</dd>
            </dl>
        </div>
    </div>
    <div id="forms" class="new-section">
        <div class="section-header">
            <h1>Forms</h1>
        </div>
        <div class="section-body">
            <form action="mailto:contact@website.com?
            subject=New %20User%20Request" method=
            "post">
```

```
            <label for="firstname">First Name:
              </label><input type="text"
              id="firstname" name="firstname">
            </br/>
            <label for="firstname">Surname:
              </label><input type="text"
              name="surname">
            <br/>
            <label for="firstname">Email: </label>
              <input type="email" name="email">
            <br/>
            <input type="submit">
          </form>
       </div>
     </div>
  </body>
</html>
```

Part Two
CSS

In the previous section we discussed the important role that HTML plays in the creation of a website. We even built our own HTML webpage, making use of the various tags that form the core of all websites we see in production today. You might have noticed that up until this point, the webpage we have created is looking rather on the basic side. A far cry from some of the more visually stimulating websites we all use on a daily basis. Well, this is where CSS (Cascading Style Sheets) come into play. CSS is responsible for styling the HTML that we write. It has the power to take our bland website and turn it into a beautifully constructed masterpiece.

CSS can completely transform a website without needing to alter the HTML at all.

4.1

Welcome to this website		Welcome to this website	
Example context	Example context	Example context	
		Example context	
Example context	Example context	Example context	
		Example context	

Welcome to this website			
Example context	Example context	Example context	Example context

In Figure 4.1 we can see three webpages with completely different styles. They are almost indistinguishable from one another. Their HTML is identical, but their CSS is vastly different. This example should help you to start to understand the power and flexibility of CSS.

This section will see us through the journey of understating the link between HTML and CSS and the possibilities that CSS affords us when creating a visual style for our webpages. We will explore how CSS works at a basic level, and its relationship with HTML. We will then dive further into the concepts and rules that form CSS, before finally moving on to constructing our own CSS code for use on the webpage we created in the previous section.

By the end of this section you will have a firm grasp on how to construct CSS code and will be well equipped with the ability to transform any webpage into a work of art.

04
CSS Part 1

What we will learn in this chapter

In this chapter we will learn how CSS works, how to construct CSS, element, id and class selectors, comment, inserting CSS, properties and links, as well as a number of core CSS concepts including the box model.

How CSS works

Before diving into the exciting prospect of making our webpage look pretty, it's important to understand exactly what CSS is and how it works. Don't worry – it's actually very simple and in no time at all we will be moving on to writing CSS code and having fun styling our webpages.

If the HTML of a webpage is a way of telling a browser *what* should be displayed on our webpage, then CSS describes to the browser *how* that content should be displayed. Let's use an example of an <h1> tag. The <h1> tag tells the browser that we would like to have a heading on the webpage: the CSS would then explain how we want that header to appear; what colour it should be; the font size; the letter spacing; if it should be centre or left aligned and many more possibilities. Looking at this example we can see just how powerful CSS can be and the possibilities it gives us.

Remember how, in the previous section, we looked at ids and classes and how we can use them as a way of targeting content? Well, you might have been wondering how and why you might want to target content. This is where the relationship between HTML and CSS comes into play. By giving a piece of content an id or class, we can write CSS rules that we apply directly to the corresponding id or class, which then in turn correlates to and styles that specific piece of content.

How to construct CSS

A style sheet can be seen as a set of instructions to the browser (eg, give this element a blue background, make this font green). In practice, it is not much more complicated than that to construct – CSS is a relatively simple language. It has its quirks, of course, but we will get into that later on.

Let's first look at an example of a CSS rule:

```
h1 {
  color: blue;
  text-align: center;
}
```

Pretty simple, right? I'm sure you can make a few assumptions as to how this works, but let's break down exactly what is going on here.

A CSS rule consists of two parts: a selector and a declaration block. The selector is where you specify which element you are targeting with your rule, while the declaration block contains the rules you wish to apply to the targeted element. Within the declaration block, which is defined using curly braces, you use name and value pairs (separated with a colon) to define your rules. These are pre-set terms that you will need to know in order to style an element effectively. You will notice that each declaration inside the declaration block ends with a semi-colon. This is essential as your CSS will 'break' if you fail to end a declaration with a semi-colon.

While there are some exceptions to this rule, it's good practice to always end your declaration with a semi-colon.

And that's all there is to it. Every CSS rule you ever write will follow this same structure of a selector and a declaration block. While the contents will change, the actual structure will always be the same. Now let's look at the selector part in more detail.

Element selector

The element selector is used to target (or 'find') HTML elements based on the value you specify. There are many ways of targeting elements depending on the criteria specified. Let's first look at a way of targeting generic tags directly. To target a tag, you simply specify the tag name, be it h1, h2, p, div, span, etc. When you specify a generic tag, every occurrence of that tag within your webpage will be styled with the rules you apply. Powerful, right? With CSS, you can write just one rule, which can change the style of that element across your entire website. Look at the following example:

```
h1 {
  color: blue;
  text-align: center;
}
```

This will see every <h1> tag updated to display the text in the colour blue and centre aligned. Looking at this simple example should help you to begin to understand just how much time CSS can save you when building websites. Imagine if you had to change the style of each <h1> element manually?

id selector

Selecting an HTML element by id is very straightforward: you simply use the specified id prefixed with a '#'. As we highlighted in the

HTML section, every id you use must be unique, and, therefore, must only ever apply to a single element. In this way, when we write a CSS rule for an id, that rule will only apply to that single element. Looking at the following example, we can see how this works in action:

HTML

```
<div id="navigation-menu">
Menu Item 1
</div>
```

CSS

```
#navigation-menu {
color: red;
text-align: left;
}
```

In this example, the one div with the id of 'navigation-menu' will have the style applied. This direct targeting approach allows us to isolate individual elements that have a unique style. This increased level of control offers us the ability to take control of and fine-tune our design as per our requirements.

Class selector

The class selector is equally as straightforward as the id selector – we just need to substitute the '#' for a '.' Selecting a class will update all HTML elements that contain that class. As explained in the HTML section, classes can and should be used across multiple elements. By adding a class to a selection of elements, you are able to target and apply a style to those elements all at once. Let's see an example of how this might be used in the wild:

HTML

```
<h1 class="centered-text">
Example Header 1
</h1>
<p>Example body text</p>
<h1 class="centered-text">
Example Header 2
</h1>
```

CSS

```
.centeredText {
text-align: center;
}
```

You can see how helpful combining classes with CSS can be. If we define a style that can be reused and applied across the website, we can simply add that class to any element in our HTML and have it instantly update to the desired style without needing to change our CSS at all. We can simply create our website style in our CSS, then build pages with HTML just adding classes to inject our styling as we wish. This keeps your webpage nice and consistent, and also speeds up the development process. Remember you can also use as many classes as you like; this way you can combine styles to form the desired effect for your element. Let's update our example to see how this can be used in practice.

HTML

```
<h1 class="centered-text blue-text">
Example Header 1
</h1>
<h1 class="centered-text blue-text">
Example Header 2
</h1>
```

CSS

```
.centered-text {
text-align: center;
}
.blue-text {
color: blue;
}
```

As you can see, we simply define our style once in our CSS and we can reuse the associated class wherever we feel appropriate across our page.

Remember, on top of this, you can also combine ids and classes to apply individual styles as well as global styles. This can be useful in situations where you want to make a tweak to a single element that is making use of a class.

Grouping selectors together

Sometimes we need to apply the same style to multiple elements, instead of doing this three separate times, like so:

CSS

```
p {
color: red;
}
h1 {
color: red;
}
h2 {
color: red;
}
```

In this situation we can actually combine these styles into one, more general, style separating our elements with a comma like so:

CSS

```
p, h1, h2 {
color: red;
}
```

This approach reduces the length of your code, improves legibility and keeps the file size of your CSS file to a minimum, which in turn will improve your page loading speed. Remember that your page loading speed should be considered and measured throughout the entire development process.

Comments

When writing code, it's useful to annotate your code with comments that explain your logic. This helps both yourself to remember why you might have written the code, and any other developers that might work on the file in the future. Comments are ignored by the browser, and are purely for documentation purposes. A comment is created using the following syntax:

```
/* Example comment
in a document */
```

You will notice that you denote the start of the comment with a /* and mark the end with a */. Comments can span on to multiple lines if necessary. It's good practice to write meaningful comments where necessary throughout your CSS file.

Inserting CSS

We have now discussed the role and syntax of CSS, but you might be wondering where and how we document our CSS to be read by the browser. Well, there are actually three different methods we can use to 'insert' our CSS into our webpage document. They each have their own uses and benefits, which we will run through now. The three methods are as follows.

External style sheet

This approach allows us to write all of our CSS code in one .css file, which we reference (link to) in our webpage. You can include this link on as many webpages as you wish. You can then simply up-date this .css file at any point and have the styles update across all of your webpages at once.

The .css file is simply a plain text file that can be created in any text-editor, saved with the .css extension, then your rules are simply listed in there without any other special syntax. Here is an example .css layout

```
.centeredText {
text-align: center;
}.
blueText {
color: blue;
}
```

We then save this file, and provide the link in the <head> tag of all the webpages we want the file to be used for. The syntax for this is as follows:

```
<head>
  <link rel="stylesheet" type="text/css" href="style.css">
</head>
```

You will notice that this tag is a self-closing tag that makes use of the res, type and href attributes. When referencing a CSS file, the res and type attributes will always remain the same. The href attribute, however, just like we have seen previously with our hyperlinks, will contain a path to your css file. Remember the usual rules of absolute/relative links apply here, so ensure that your path is correct if you nest your .css file within a subfolder.

This approach is favourable as it keeps the codebase in one single file which makes writing and maintaining the CSS code much easier going forward. It also means we only have to update our code in one place and have it propagate across multiple webpages. This approach does have its drawbacks, however, and is not always ideal, or necessary. Having the css file as a separate resource means that the browser has to request an additional asset (the .css file), which will have a small impact on the speed at which your page loads. Though this difference may be incredibly small, milliseconds can really count on larger production websites.

Internal style sheet

Internal style sheets are used for embedding CSS rules directly to a webpage. This is useful if your webpage has a small number of rules that apply only to that page; instead of including the unique styles in the main css file that is used across your entire website, you can save space in your .css file by moving these unique styles directly into the relevant webpage. This is nice and simple to do as well – we simply add an opening and closing HTML <style> tag to the head of our webpage and put our styles in there. An example can be seen below:

```
<head>
  <style>
    h1 {
    color: blue;
    font-size: 14px;
    }
  </style>
</head>
```

Inline styles

Inline styles are used to apply a style directly to an element within the HTML tag itself. This approach makes use of the style attribute of HTML tags to apply the style direct. While this approach is the fastest in terms of time taken to render the style, as no 'lookup' is required (no need for a selector), using this method and mixing HTML with CSS can mean that your webpage becomes confusing to code and analyse. You also lose the advantage of reusable styles and the simplicity of a single codebase for your CSS.

Let's see how this approach works in practice:

```
<h1 style="color:green;font-size:12px;">Example
heading</h1>
```

This approach works identically to any other HTML attribute, in the sense that it follows the same pattern of: attributename= "attributeValue"

You will notice how you can chain multiple styles together after each semi-colon. As the style is inline and applied directly to the element, we don't need a selector or any curly braces. This approach can become extremely messy, very quickly, especially when working on elements with multiple style rules. Use this approach sparingly, if at all.

Exercise

We've learned a lot in this section already so you're now well on your way to understanding all you need to know about CSS. It's a good time to put your skills to the test and set up our environment for the subsequent sections where we will be exploring a few of the CSS properties that we will be using when building our website later on in this book.

So let's start by creating the link required for this. We're going to need a global css file that will be used on all of our webpages, so start by creating a file named main.css that exists inside a folder called 'styles' in our root directory; link this css file to our existing webpages. Then, inside the css file, set the colour of all <h1> tags to blue. We have covered how to do this already – just read back through the sections if you get stuck.

Core concepts

While the syntax of CSS is nice and simple, there are a few areas of CSS that can get a little bit more challenging to understand, but don't worry, we will break them down now and by the end of this section you will have a firm grasp on these concepts, and you will be well on your way to mastering CSS. We will be styling those webpages you created in the last chapter in no time at all.

Inheritance

Let's start with a conversion around a core principle of CSS, inheritance. While the term itself might suggest that this concept is going to be a confusing and advanced principle, it's actually relatively simple. To understand it, we first need to understand a bit more about how a webpage is rendered. As we saw already when we were building the HTML for our webpage, everything inside a webpage is nested within another element; for example, the <script> tag is nested inside the <head> tag, which is nested within the <html> tag along with the rest of the website. Well, this structure is hugely important to how our webpage, and our CSS operates.

When our created webpage is loaded by a browser, the browser analyses the HTML and creates an 'object' based on your HTML structure. This is called the DOM (document object model), you can think of the DOM as a reverse tree-like structural representation of your webpage, where elements can have parents, children and siblings. See Figure 4.2 below for reference of a visual example of a DOM structure.

4.2

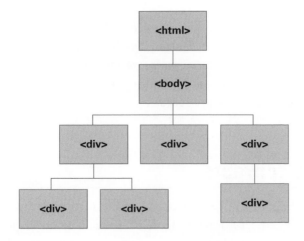

Now if you analyse this tree structure, you will see how <body> is a 'child' of <html>, and <body> is also a parent of all of your actual document, which contains a lot of siblings, which have children of their own, etc. This orderly approach of nested elements allows us to make use of inheritance in CSS.

Inheritance works just like it does in real life. A child can inherit attributes from its parent and share some attributes with its siblings. In HTML, it's important to note that an element will only ever have one parent. But the principle remains the same.

Let's look at an example. If I applied a style to the <body> element, every child of the <body> element would also receive the style. So if I gave the body a property of colour – green – all of the text in the children elements would also be green, unless this is overridden (more on that later). There are some styles that don't get passed down in the same way as the colour property does, such as the border property. Welcome to the world of CSS. There are many of these small quirks that you will become accustomed to over time. In any case, the simple concept of a parent sharing its attributes with its children elements is the principle of inheritance. See, that wasn't so bad was it?

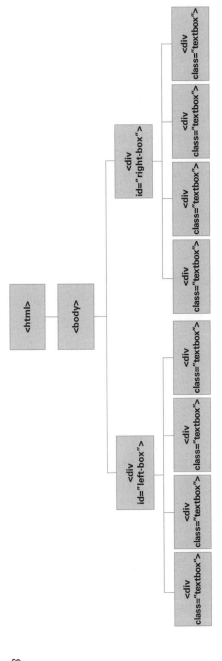

4.3

Nesting

Following on from our discussion around inheritance, let's quickly assess the possibilities this opens up for how we target attributes with CSS.

In CSS you can nest your selectors in order to finely choose which element to select. Let's take the document structure in Figure 4.3 as an example.

You will notice we have eight divs with the class 'textbox' in Figure 4.3, four of which have a parent with an id 'left-box' and four with a parent with the id 'right-box'. Let's say we only want to apply styles to the divs with the class 'textbox' that sit within the 'left-box' div, well with CSS we can do that. We simply nest the elements in the selector like so:

```
#left-box .text-box {
color: red;
}
```

This will now target only the divs with the class text-box, if they also have a parent with the id of left-box. This allows us ultimate flexibility and control over how we target and select elements to style.

Cascading

When working with CSS it is quite likely that you will run into a situation where you have conflicting styles operating on an element. For example, if you had a div with multiple classes applied to it with a conflicting property, like in the following example:

HTML

```
<div id="navigation" class="blueBackground
redBackground">
```

CSS

```
#navigation {
background: yellow;
}
.blueBackground {
background: blue;
}
.redBackground {
background: red;
}
```

This setup creates a situation where the browser needs to establish which value for the 'background' rule should be honoured as the most important one. Enter the cascading nature of CSS.

In these situations where a conflict is apparent on an element, the browser will look at the circumstances of the styles, and decide which has more 'priority'. Let's take a look at how priority is deemed with CSS.

First the browser will look at how the style is applied to the element and apply a weighting system based on this. From most to least important, the cascading system looks something like this:

- *Inline styles.* Inline styles are deemed the most important element and will almost always have top priority in the event of a conflict. Because the style is applied directly to the element, the browser assumes that this is the style that you intend to have operating on the element, and as such this is the style from which the conflicting property will be selected.

- *External/internal style sheets.* If no inline styles are applied to the element, then the browser will choose the property from the external/internal file (in this case, the internal file means the code in the style tag in the head of the document). In this case the browser will also apply a system of weighting based on the last occurring property in the document. For example, if I had two conflicting class styles defined on an element, the browser would go through the CSS file and look for the last occurrence of that conflicting property and use that. Therefore, if the style is defined lower down in the document, it is deemed more important, and therefore honoured. Likewise, if the style tag is used in the head section *after* the link tag referencing the stylesheet, then that internal sheet will be deemed more important, and within that internal sheet, the same principles apply, of lower down means more important.

- *Browser default.* Remember when we first generated our HTML in Chapter 2 and the browser outputted some default styling, for example our <h1> tags were bold and given a larger font size than our <p> tags? Well, this was the work of what we call a browser default. To help us out a bit, browsers come shipped with standard styles for commonly used HTML elements, such as text elements, where the browser will default to a helpful style in line with the nature of the tag. If no other style is operating on an element, this is what the browser will use to render your content.

A note about !important

While the above cascading rules operate on all content, there is a way to override this, which can be particularly useful as a method of asserting style dominance. We can make use of the !important indicator as a method of protecting a style from being overridden regardless of where the style appears next. Even if a CSS rule is conflicting with one further down the document, the !important rule will still be honoured. Let's see how this works:

```
p {
color: red !important;
}
```

This is a bit different to anything we have seen so far, but it's nice and easy to understand. We simply add the !important suffix to a rule in our CSS, and that ensures the rule will not be overridden. The only exception to this is where another rule, later on in the document, also has the important indicator. In this case, the usual rules apply of which one has more dominance in the cascading chain. As a general rule, it's best to avoid using !important unless we are absolutely certain that the style should never be overridden. Developing on a CSS file where !important has been used can be problematic on large long-term projects.

The box model

If there's one concept that underpins every aspect of CSS, it has to be the box model concept. The box model helps us to understand how our webpage renders elements, and helps us to have more control over how we can structure our webpage to achieve our desired layout. By understanding the box model, you will gain a solid foundation and understanding of how HTML is handled by the browser, which will help you on your way to becoming a professional web developer.

In its simplest form, the box model stipulates that each and every HTML element is a box. That's right, everything, even text, is a box. While at first this might seem somewhat mysterious that an element as unruly as text can be considered a box, when we analyse the benefits we get from the fact that everything is 'boxed', it's clear to see how useful it actually is. Let's look at what we can do with these elements now that we know they are all simply boxes on a page.

A box in HTML consists of four parts, which you can use at your own will – you don't have to make use of any of these parts, you can simply leave the content as a box and so be it, as you have seen so far, the box itself is hidden by default. So what are these four parts? Content, padding, border, margin.

I'm sure you've already made some assumptions around how these four parts work, but you might be surprised. Figure 4.4 provides a visual representation.

4.4

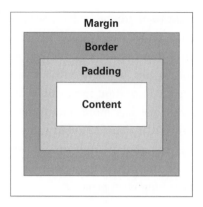

- *Content.* This one is completely self-explanatory. The content is the contents of the box, the text, image, list, whatever you are trying to display, this is your content.

- *Padding.* Think of padding as the gap between your content and the edge of your box. Padding is always transparent. Imagine it as a way of giving space between your content and the surrounding box.

- *Border.* The line around your box, the box itself, it goes around the padding and its enclosed content and tightly wraps around your box.

- *Margin.* Margin can be seen as the space around your box. Just like the padding it is transparent, only this time it is clearing space around your box and other elements, not your content.

As you probably expect, all of these parts can be tweaked as per your requirements. You can give a box a lot of padding and a thick border, you can give a huge margin to ensure your box sits in isolation and you can choose how your content displays with the usual properties, such as colour, etc.

Thinking of our HTML elements as boxes allows us to understand how our page fits together and how we can take control of our content and output it exactly as we wish. It's extremely powerful.

Seeing it in action

Well done: you have just worked your way through some new and challenging, but extremely important, concepts. Having a firm grasp on these concepts is crucial to ensuring that your experience with CSS is as smooth as possible.

The good news is that we're now finished with concepts for this chapter. From here on in it's just a case of getting familiar with the various rules we can apply to our styles. Before we jump ahead and start playing about with the potential rules we can make use of, let's solidify our understanding and see how we can put what we've learned into action.

I'm about to introduce you to your new best friend as a budding web developer. It lives inside Google Chrome and goes by the alias of the 'inspector tool'. The inspector tool is a powerful debugging feature built into Google Chrome which allows web developers to 'inspect' a webpage to see a visual representation of how the page is made up. Inspector tools will show you the invisible boxes around your elements. To see it in action you must first right-click any element on a webpage and click 'Inspect'. You will see a snapshot of the HTML code constructing the element along with the associated CSS code operating on that element. Hovering over any element in the HTML tree view will highlight that element on the page, with a representation of the box that engulfs the content too.

4.5

```
[☐ ⓘ]  Elements  Console  Sources  Network  Performance  Memory  Application  Security  Audits  Redux  AdBlock
   ▼<section id="home" data-speed="10" data-type="background">
   ▶<div id="homeInner" style="height: 734px;">…</div> == $0
   </section>
   ▼<div id="wrap">
      ▼<div class="container">
         <div class="clear"></div>
         ▼<div id="header" class="sixteen columns clearfix">
            ::before
            <div class="inner">
            </div>
            ::after
         </div>
         <div class="clear"></div>
         ▶<div id="navigation" class="sixteen columns clearfix">…</div>
   html.js.no-touch   body.html.front.not-logged-in.no-sidebars.page-node.page-node-.page-node-2.node-type-page.lightbox-processed.responsiv
```

Its uses don't stop there, though. When using inspector tools during the building phase of your webpage, instead of having to save your .html file and reload the webpage in your browser each time you want to test out a change, you can simply manipulate the CSS and HTML code direct in your browser and see it change in real time. This saves a developer an unfathomable amount of time when developing.

Why not take some time to get familiar with your new best friend? You're going to be seeing a lot more of it in the future.

Properties

Now that we are familiar with the mechanics and syntax of CSS, it's time to get to the exciting part that you've been waiting for: the magic properties that are going to be responsible for transforming your HTML from simple content into an actual design like those we see every day online. Let's jump right in and explore the options we have for styling text.

For this section we will be looking in detail at the various properties we can use in CSS. For each property we will look at the exact term used for the property name itself and then we will break down the values, or types of values, that the property is expecting and will accept.

Text

Color

Let's start with the example we've been using throughout – colours, or more specifically and importantly 'color'. In CSS color and colour are not the same thing, and only one will actually work in the browser. When dealing with any colour-related property in web design, it will always be the Americanized 'color' that you will need to use. It's just the way it is, and that's that.

So now we know the property name 'color', what are the values that the property will accept? Well, we can actually specify colour in a number of ways. Let's take a closer look.

Named colours

There are a number of specified 'standard' colours that we can make use of, as we've seen so far: red, blue, green, orange, etc. These will all render the expected colour, but you might not like the tone or shade the browser chooses for you. It's unusual for a developer or designer to rely on the standard named colours for any aspect of a build (apart from for test purposes where the standard colours just have the purpose of being a quick colour to highlight an area of the page).

In reality, you are going to want to specify exactly what colour you want to use, and this is where HEX and RGB (or RGBA) values come into play. To the uninitiated, HEX and RBG values are text-based representations of a specific colour. For example, the HEX #000000 is black and #ffffff is white.

If you use any photo editing suite such as Photoshop, you will be able to grab the HEX or RGB value for a colour of your choosing. Feel free to do a Google search for HEX colours if you want some to use for testing purposes. This property also accepts RGBA values. RGBA values are identical to RGB values, only the A stands for the alpha channel, which allows us to set an opacity for the colour.

Let's see some examples and move on to some other font properties we can make use of.

```
p {
color: red;
color: #ffffff;
color: rgb(255, 0, 0);
}
```

Font-family

Fonts are selected and applied to selectors via the font-family property.

By default the available fonts that can be used in web design are somewhat limited. There's a small set of fonts that are deemed 'web safe fonts'. These are fonts that are widely supported in various browsers, and are deemed suitable for web. The issue we have here is that if a browser doesn't support a font, it must select another similar one, but we need to tell it which one. This is where the 'fallback' system comes into play.

The font-family property supports multiple values, separated by a comma, for example:

```
p {
    font-family: "Times New Roman", Times, serif;
}
```

This is saying to the browser, 'Use Times New Roman if you can; if not, use a Times font. If you can't do that, then just display a serif font.'

You can find a full list of available web-safe fonts at https://www.w3schools.com/cssref/css_websafe_fonts.asp

Font-style

The font-style property is seldom used for anything other than forcing text into being rendered in italics. The property has only three available values: normal, italic and oblique. Normal is the default browser style for all text, italic will set the text to render in italics and oblique is very similar to italics but not as severe.

This one is nice and simple and can be used in the following way:

```
p {
  font-style: italic;
}
```

Font-size

This one is a nice and descriptive property, which really speaks for itself; needless to say, this is how we set the size of the font. The font size can be set in a number of ways, which we will touch more on later, but for now, let's use the absolute method of using px (pixels) to set the font size:

```
h1 {
  font-size: 40px;
}
```

This will give the font a height of 40px.

Font weight

Font weight is how we describe the weight or body of the text. In simple terms, we are looking at how thick the font is. The values here can be as follows: normal, light, lighter, bold, semi-bold. But also numerical values such as 100, 300, 500, 700.

Each font has different weights that can be assigned to it, which can be seen at the link referenced earlier. An example of how this is used in a CSS document is as follows:

```
p.thick {
  font-weight: bold;
}
```

Font variant

Font variant is responsible for applying an override on the case of the font, for example we can make all text uppercase, or lowercase, or small-caps, which contains uppercase letters that appear smaller in font size than the original version.

The syntax for this is as follows:

```
p {
    font-variant: small-caps;
}
```

Links

Styling links

Styling links is just like styling normal text. We can use all of the same properties that we can for normal text (colour, background, font size, etc), but we also get access to some modifiers that allow us to directly target the state of the link. Let's look first at styling a standard link.

```
a {
color: red;
}
```

Simple enough – we just use the tag name (a) to highlight all links. Nothing new here, we are simply adding a style to a tag. Now let's take things a step further by styling the text differently when the user hovers over the link.

```
a:hover {
color: blue;
}
```

You will notice that we have added on a state modifier with the ':hover'. This code now means that whenever we hover over the link, the text will turn blue. There are four states in total that we can watch out for. They are:

- a:link. This is a standard, **unvisited** link.

- a:visited. This state will target links that have already been visited by the user.

- a:hover. This state will target links that are currently being hovered over by the user's mouse.

- a:active. This state is for when a user clicks on the link, that exact moment is the active state and lasts for a very short period

By using these states we are able to enhance our websites and convey extra meaning to our users about the links on our website.

What we have learned in this chapter

Now that we have covered the essentials of CSS and a number of crucial concepts, Chapter 5 will build upon this knowledge as we look at colour, borders, margins, padding, floats and more about the box model.

05
CSS Part 2

What we will learn in this chapter

This chapter will cover more exciting ways to use CSS, through colour, borders, margins, padding, floats and more.

Colour

Let's move on now to something a bit more exciting. Colour, or more precisely, using colours on webpages. Colour is everywhere online and its uses are endless. It can be used to add emphasis to important information, break up the flow of a webpage, reflect corporate branding, incite emotion, tell a story or simply just indicate that an element can be clicked. Thankfully, as a developer, adding colour to your website is a fairly straightforward affair. Using colour *effectively* on your webpage – well, that's a little bit more challenging. This section will show us how to apply colour to our HTML elements. Along the journey we will also look at some professional tips for using colour effectively in our webpages through some real-world examples.

Background

Background colour

As with a lot of CSS attributes, background colour somewhat speaks for itself. It literally applies a colour of your choosing to the background of an element. Remembering what we've already learned about colour, we can apply colour using any of the methods specified (hex, rgba, keyword).

It is important to understand that this property will only change the colour of the background *inside* the element. Remembering the box model concept, this means that any padding will be coloured too, but any margin applied to the element will not. Borders also exist outside the box, so they would not be affected either. Let's see this in action:

HTML

```
<div id="box">
Some information
</div>
```

CSS

```
#box {
background-color: #000000;
color: #ffffff;
}
```

Result:

Some information

As you can see, the background has been made black, as per the hex code applied to the background-colour property. Also the text has been made white by the hex code used for 'color'. This use of opposing colours against one another (white against its contrasting colour black) is one of the most important theories to consider when choosing colours for your website. Using contrasting colours helps to ensure that text can be read with ease by your users. Choosing colours that are closer to each other in the colour spectrum often produces issues of legibility for your users.

Background image

Background images are images that are applied to the entire background of an element. One of the main benefits of background images over a standard image is that you can overlay text with ease over the top of the background image, and it is also a little bit easier to manipulate the image than when using the standard image element. Let's explore:

First, the syntax. The syntax for adding a background image to an element is as follows:

CSS

```
background-image: url("image.png");
```

As usual, if you use a PNG image, the browser will consider the transparency settings of the image. So if you have an icon without a background, for example, the image will sit nicely over any colour you have behind it without any issues. This can be extremely powerful. If you were to apply a background-colour property to an element and also a background-image, the background image would appear over the top of the background colour, allowing you to 'layer' your background as you wish. This is an extremely powerful technique for creating unique backgrounds. The syntax for this rule is slightly different to anything we have seen before. We have a hyphenated property 'background-image' and the value contains a keyword 'url', brackets and speech marks. This might seem bizarre at first as it is so different from how we write other rules, but it's actually fairly simple. The biggest consideration here is how to format your URL. As with HTML you can specify your URL in either absolute or relative terms. Remember, if you use a relative path, this will search for your image relative to the location of your CSS file, not your HTML webpage that you attach the CSS file to inside the <head>tag.

Background-repeat

When using a background image, if the image is smaller than the size of the element it is used on, the image will repeat to cover the entire size of the element, as shown in Figure 5.1.

5.1

This is where the background-repeat property comes into use. We are able to apply any of the following values to the property in order to control the repeating nature of the background image.

no-repeat

The background image will not repeat at all, regardless of the size of either the image or the element (see Figure 5.2).

5.2

repeat-x

The background image will only repeat horizontally, but will still repeat until the full width of the div is covered with the image (see Figure 5.3).

5.3

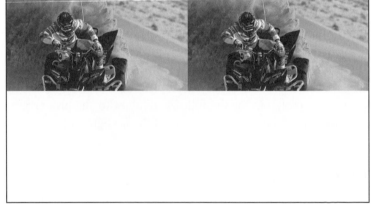

repeat-y

The background image will only repeat vertically, but will still repeat until the full height of the div is covered with the image (Figure 5.4).

5.4

Background-position

The background-position property does pretty much exactly what you would expect it to do – positions the background image as per your specified value.

Generally you would provide two values for this property – the horizontal and vertical values – to define where you want the image to be positioned inside your element. A classic example of this would be as follows:

```
.background-div {
background-image: url("image.png");
background-repeat: no-repeat;
background-position: centre bottom;
}
```

5.5

As you can see from the above example, the image moves to the corresponding location based on our inputted value. Simple, right? Well, here's where it gets a little more powerful and thus a bit more complicated. CSS allows us three different ways to specify the position for these values. They are as follows…

By keyword

The keyword values are left, centre, right, top and bottom. These keywords will always force the image to the furthermost point specified. For example, the keyword 'left' will force the image to the far left of the element (Figure 5.6).

```
.background-div {
background-image: url("image.png");
background-repeat: no-repeat;
background-position: left;
}
```

5.6

By percentage

Defining the image's position by percentage is used to outline how far away from the corresponding edge the image must be. If we look at a typical div element, the far left side would be 0 per cent, and the far right would be 100 per cent, thus 50 per cent is in the direct centre of the div and 75 per cent is three-quarters of the way along the div. The same system applies for the vertical measurement as well. 0 per cent is the top of the div, 100 per cent is the bottom of the div. You can quickly see how much control over our image's placement this gives us in a very easy to use way. By contrast, positioning a standard image element can be particularly cumbersome at times.

```
.background-div {
background-image: url("image.png");
background-repeat: no-repeat;
background-position: 50% 70%;
}
```

5.7

By measurements

We can also simply use pixels as a unit of measurement for specifying where our image should reside. We can simply state in pixels exactly how far along from the edge the image must be, and that is where the image will move along to. As we can see in the below example:

```
.background-div {
background-image: url("image.png");
background-repeat: no-repeat;
background-position: 100px 50px;
}
```

5.8

And that's all there is to it. Three simple but powerful ways to manipulate the position of our background image.

Just as a quick side-note, by default the background-position property has the value 'center' for both horizontal and vertical alignments. Also, if you leave off the vertical value for the property, the vertical alignment will be assumed to be 'center' too, as we can see in Figure 5.9.

5.9

This background-position property is a very powerful one that has a lot of use in the real world, so it's important to understand it fully. Let's work on an example together to put the valuable skills we just learned into practice.

Exercise

We are going to be creating an 'icon' type div that could be used on our homepage as a quick link to another page on our website. Using the background-image manipulation techniques we have learned above:

1 Create a new div on your index.html file and give them each a class of 'navigation-card'.
2 Inside our CSS file add the appropriate rules for the class to add the 'exampleicon.png' file from the images folder on to the divs.
3 Make sure that the image doesn't repeat.
4 Place the image in the centre of the div.
5 Give the class a height of 150px and a width of 150px.

The final output should look something like Figure 5.10.

5.10

Background attachment

Background attachment introduces a new concept that we haven't seen before. This concept is fixed positioning. Fixed positioning is where an element on a webpage remains where it is regardless of where the user has scrolled. The best way to understand this is to see it in action. Let's run through a quick exercise to highlight exactly what we mean when we say fixed positioning. First, open up your CSS file in your text editor of choice, then add the following snippet to the end of your code:

```
body {
height: 2000px;
background: url('exampleicon.png') no-repeat;
background-attachment: fixed;
border: 1px solid black;
}
```

Save the file and open up your index.html page in Google Chrome. Scroll the page down and look at what happens to the icons you added to the body. Notice how they remained in the same place while the rest of the page scrolled down? This is how fixed positioning works in web design.

This example highlights the power and flexibility that this property allows developers. The ability to separate out fixed elements from the rest of the page like this allows a developer opportunities that are simply not possible if every element is bound to the scroll of a webpage.

Background image

That about draws a close to the background image related properties, but before we move on, you need to be aware of a method used to speed up setting these various properties and values – ready for when you're more familiar with how each of them works and will be using them in a real-world environment.

This is the 'background' property. Imagine if we rolled up all of the 'background' related properties into one 'super' property which allowed you to easily choose which values to set and in any order you liked. Well, that is exactly what the background property does. Let's see its simplistic beauty in action.

Thanks to the wonderful background property, this hefty chunk of code:

```
.background-div {
background-color: red;
background-image: url("image.png");
background-repeat: no-repeat;
background-position: right bottom;
background-attachment: fixed;
}
```

becomes this:

```
.background-div {
background: red url("image.png") no-repeat right bottom
fixed;
}
```

Not only does this speed up page load due to the decrease in size of the css (less lines of code = smaller file size, remember), it also speeds up development time as the developer doesn't need to enter each of the property names individually.

The only restriction imposed on the order of the property values is the horizontal then vertical condition of the background-position value; other than that, the values can be entered in any order at all. Trust me – this speeds up development more than you can possibly imagine.

The box model part 2

We've already discussed the importance of the box model. Here is where we can start to see the concept in use a little bit more. Let's take another look at the makeup of an element in HTML (see Figure 5.11).

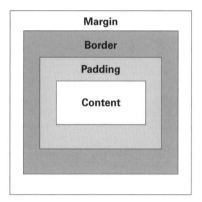

Familiarizing yourself with this visual representation will help you to understand the upcoming parts of this section. Got it? Great, now let's look at setting the size of an element.

Widths and heights

If you cast your mind back to when we rendered our first image back in Chapter 3, you might remember we saw the width and height properties that we applied directly to the image. Well, these are the same properties we use for sizing all elements using CSS too, just simply 'width' and 'height'. The values for the width and height can be specified in length (pixel, em, etc) or percentage formats, like so:

```
.background-div {
width: 50%;
height: 100px;
}
```

Setting the width or height will update the content of the element only, not the padding or the margin.

When specifying the value as a percentage, the element will be set to that percentage width of its direct parent element. Figure 5.12 is an example of this.

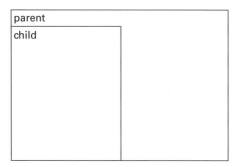

The height and width properties have a few quirks that take a while to get used to. For example, you can specify to set the width of an element to be 100 per cent of the parent and it will work as expected, but it will not work in the same way with the height property. The width property also can't be applied to inline elements, such as hyperlinks, without first converting the element into a block element (more on that later).

On this note, there are many quirks in HTML and CSS that might seem strange at first, but in time you will come to appreciate the quirks more and understand that they are actually by design and help the developer rather than hinder them. Hang in there new developers – it will all make sense eventually.

Borders, padding and margins

In this section we'll look at borders, padding and margins. They form the makeup of all block-level elements and provide us with a lot of flexibility when outlining our structure.

Borders

As I explained in the previous chapter, the border is the line around the element that wraps up your content and padding, but not your margin. It's the boundary of your element, really. Just like, you know, a border. You might have noticed by now that CSS and HTML tags and properties can be extremely descriptive at times. This can be a great help when first starting out in web design.

So – borders – what can we do with them? Well, actually quite a lot. Let's start by looking at all the different styles of borders we can apply:

- *Dotted.* A dotted border.
- *Dashed.* A longer, dashed border.
- *Solid.* A solid border without anything fancy.
- *Double.* A double lined border.
- *Groove.* A 3D grooved border.
- *Ridge.* A 3D ridged border.
- *Inset.* A 3D grooved border.
- *Outset.* A 3D grooved border.
- *Hidden.* Hides the border but keeps the space.

Let's run through a quick exercise to familiarize yourself with how each of the styles renders in the browser.

Exercise

Make a copy of your lists.html page, name it 'borders.html' and strip out all content inside the .content div. Inside here create a new div with a class of 'border-test' then in your CSS file add the following style:

```
.border-test {
width: 200px;
height: 100px;
border-style: dotted;
}
```

Save both files and open borders.html in Google Chrome.
Notice our lovely dotted border? Now substitute the 'dotted'
value out for some of the other styles and get a feel for how
each one renders. There are some very useful effects that you
might have seen in use across the web before. Once you have
finished this exercise, keep the new file. We will revisit it later
on in this chapter.

Border-width

Now that you've got the excitement of playing around with border
styles out of your system, it's time to move swiftly on to the border-
width property. This one is another gem from the self-explanatory
nature of CSS, but for clarity let's address the property with appropriate respect as it does have some useful and interesting values.

Example:

```
.border-test {
width: 200px;
height: 100px;
border-style: dotted;
border-width: 2px;
}
```

As you probably expected, widths can be set with length values, such as px, pt, em, etc, but it also accepts three pre-defined values: thin, medium and thick. The browser will handle the rendering of these three values, so I'll leave it to a combination of your curiosity and the borders.html file for you to find out how the browser handles the pre-defined values.

Border-color

Border-color is a nice and flexible property, which allows us to set the colour of the border. We can use the same ways of setting colour as usual, be it with name values (red, orange, blue), hex value (#ffffff) or RGB (rgb(255,255,255)). That's about all there is to say about border-color – it's a nice and easy one to use and always affords us great flexibility.

Borders – differing sides

In the above sections we have seen plenty of examples where we have applied a border to an element with great success. Well, you can also apply differing border styles, weights and colours to each *side* of the element. There are plenty of different ways to do it. Let's explore.

All of the border properties can be applied to any single side of the border with great ease. Take the example of the border-style property: as we have seen already, we can apply a border style to the whole element like so:

```
.border-test {
width: 200px;
height: 100px;
border-style: dotted;
}
```

Well, we can also break out the border style and apply it directly to individual sides like this:

```
.border-test {
width: 200px;
height: 100px;
border-top-style: dotted;
border-right-style: solid;
border-bottom-style: dotted;
border-left-style: solid;
}
```

Which will produce the following output:

5.13

Now, to make things even more exciting, we can also apply this same border style in the following way:

```
.border-test {
width: 200px;
height: 100px;
border-style: dotted solid dotted solid;
}
```

This might confuse you at first, but it actually makes a lot of sense. See, the border-related properties allow us to specify the style for each side of the border by specifying the desired style in the following order: top right bottom left, as if working your way around the box clockwise. So in our example the top and bottom would be dotted, but the sides would be solid.

We can actually take this simplifying act one step further and leave off the last two values, like so:

```
border-style: dotted solid;
```

We can do this because when specifying the values for border, the omitted values will be inherited from their opposite member, so if you leave off the bottom value, it will be copied from the top value, and likewise for the left and right values. In our example we have specified the top and the right value, therefore the browser can assume the bottom and the left value from the values we inputted. Helpful, right? We can take this principle and apply it to all of the border-related properties, and what's more, we can actually take this one step further too. Let's now look at the shorthand border property that can save us a lot of time with all of this repetition.

Shorthand border property

Remember the shorthand background property, which neatly wrapped up all of the background related properties and put them into one handy 'background' property for us to use? Well, that same level of convenience is given to us when working with borders. Let's take a look at how it works.

Just as before, it's just a single word property. In this case, it's just 'border', but the property takes on multiple values. So we can pass in border-width, border-style and border-colour all in one go. Just like so:

```
border: 5px solid red;
```

These values can be input in any order, and aside from the border-style property (which is required) can be omitted if desired. We can also use the shorthand property for individual sides of the element, like so:

```
border-left: 5px solid red;
border-bottom: 5px solid red;
```

The above example will only show the border for the top and bottom sides of the box. When specifying individual sides as the property, rather than value, the browser does not assume from its opposite side – it must be set manually.

Border-radius

Let's finish our discussion of borders with probably the most enjoyable property of all of the border-related properties: the border-radius property. Border-radius lets us specify how rounded we would like the borders of our element to be. It takes a value in either length or percentage. This property can produce wonderful results and can even allow us to render circles with pure CSS, which once was not possible at all on websites. Let's see how it works and then we can finish off the entire border conversation with a quick exercise where we can manipulate the border-radius property to turn a square box into a nicely rounded box.

First, how it works. Just as with the other border properties, we can specify all the sides in one property; the only difference this time is instead of the first value being the top, it is now the top-left corner. The principle is still the same, working our way around the box clockwise.

Let's see a couple of examples:

```
border: 5px solid red;
border-radius: 5px;
```

```
border: 5px solid red;
border-radius: 10px 5px 2px 0px;
```

Just as with the other properties, we can also specify single corners if we only want the style to appear on one, like so:

```
border: 5px solid red;
border-top-left-radius: 10px;
```

Exercise

We are now going to take what we have learned about CSS so far and put it into practice to create a rounded profile image for use on our websites:

1   Create a new div with the id of 'profile-Image'.
2   Open your CSS file in your text editor.
3   Create a new CSS rule for your div.
4   Give the div a height and width of 200px.
5   Set the background colour to white.
6   Set the background image to the profile-icon.png image in the images folder.
7   Set the background image to appear in the centre and to not repeat.
8   Give the div a solid 3px wide border in the hex colour #cccccc.
9   Round all of the corners of the div to 50 per cent.

You should have ended up with a profile image inside a circle with a border. This is a clean way of showing a profile image on a website. Your final output should look like Figure 5.14.

Congratulations on getting through the borders section. It's not as easy as it sounded, right? CSS can be deceptively difficult at times, but do stick with it. It all becomes second nature in no time at all, and your commitment will be rewarded as you start to notice your speed of development increase with every mistake you make, from which you learn more every time.

Margins

We know at this point that a margin is the space that surrounds our element, but what exactly does that mean? Well, a margin is the amount of space that is reserved around your element. It is a way of saying 'make sure no other element comes this close to me'. It helps us to structure our content and give space to our elements. Margins flow all around our element, top, bottom, left and right, the same values we saw on the border properties. They behave in a somewhat similar way, with some good old CSS quirks in there for good measure, of course.

The margin property doesn't have all of the related properties that border does; there's no 'margin-color' or margin-style' to contend with. Just the margin location properties for each side. They are as follows: margin-left, margin-right, margin-top, margin-bottom.

All of these properties can be set with length units (px, em, etc) or percentages. You can also set the property to 'auto', which is the default (more on that later).

The property is nice and simple to use. Just choose a side you want other elements to stay well clear of, and tell them how far away they need to be. In the below example we are stating that any element which comes close to the right side of the div must be at least 20px away:

```
margin-right: 20px;
```

5.15

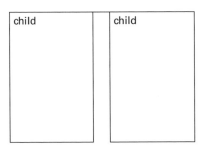

You can add any combination of the four different margins to your element, top, and bottom, top and right, right and left, etc.

Nice and simple, right? Well, it gets even easier, just like with border and background, we get an easy margin property to wrap this all up in. It works exactly as you would expect. The margin property keyword, followed by values for top, right, bottom and left, like so:

```
margin: 20px 0px 10px 0px;
```

A note about percentages

When using percentages to specify the margin, it's helpful to understand what the percentage corresponds to. In this case, the percentage specifies a margin of the width of the containing element. In the following example the margin for the nested element would be 30px:

```
margin-left: 10%;
```

16

width = 300px

margin-left = 10%

A note about negative values

Interestingly, and something we haven't seen before, when specifying margin, you can actually specify negative values. This will draw in nearby content by the amount specified. In the below example the div to the right is being sucked in by 30px in the direction that the margin has been applied.

```
margin-right: -30px;
```

5.17

It's important to understand that when considering the amount that the element is moved by, the browser takes into consideration the margin set on the target element. Looking at the following example highlights this in more detail.

5.18

margin-right = −30px	margin-left = 30px

As you can see, the left div has a margin-right of −30px, which will pull the div directly to its right in by 30px; however, the right div has a margin-left of 30px, which pushes it out again by 30px, meaning that the div is back to its original starting position as the two rules cancel each other out.

Padding

Let's finish our look at the box model with a nice and easy property, padding. As we discussed earlier in the section, padding relates to the space between your content and your border. It is often used to add a bit of 'breathing space' around your content to allow for easier reading of your text. The padding property doesn't throw up anything that we haven't seen before; as you can tell from the general pattern of these properties, we have the more declarative form and the shorthand form for each. Padding is no different. First the declarative forms:

padding-top

padding-right

padding-bottom

padding-left

Just as with the other box-related properties, we can specify the property value using length values or as a percentage (again, as a percentage of the containing element). Then, as expected, we also have the shorthand padding property, on which we are able to specify our individual sides padding values in the usual clockwise order, like so:

```
padding: 20px 0px 10px 0px;
```

As with the margin property, we can leave off as many properties as we wish (one is a minimum) and the rest will be assumed from their opposite side (if specified, otherwise the main value will be used).

From 'the box model' to 'our box model'

We have now explored the depths of the fundamental concept of the box model and welcomed it into our hearts. You should be proud of yourself – this is no easy feat. The box model underpins the design and layout of all HTML elements and understanding it fully will serve you well in your web developing years to come. Before we move on to the next quirky corner of CSS, let's have a quick recap of the box model to ensure we really do understand this concept:

- The box model applies to all HTML elements.

- Content is at the core of all elements.

- Widths and heights are applied to the content.

- Padding sits between the content and the border.

- Borders sit between padding and margins.

- Borders can have multiple styles used on different sides of the element.

- Borders can allow us to round off the corners of an element.

- Margins sit outside our element and push or pull other elements in.

- Margins can be negative in value.

- Border, margin and padding all have shorthand values as well as their more declarative counterparts.

If any of these concepts tripped you up, don't worry, just keep on working your way through the book. There will be plenty of opportunities to use the concepts above in an attempt to further familiarize yourself with the properties. Hang in there – all developers were once new to the industry and struggled with at least one concept in their early days. It's all part of growing to become a better developer.

Floats

Floats tend to be a bit tricky for new developers as it introduces a new way of thinking about layouts that most people would not have encountered before in real life or digitally, but it's actually quite simple. Remember how by default, all block-level elements start on a new line? Well, floats are a way for us to tell a browser which pieces of content should break from this format and be placed next to each other. It's easier to show you rather than explain, so let's see some examples.

First, we'll look at how to use the float property. We can use the float property with any of the following values: left, right and none.

```
float: left;
```

Now let's see some examples of how this works. In the following example, we have two block-level image elements, which by default are rendered on top of one another. Remember, this is the standard behaviour for block-level elements.

.19

Obviously this isn't ideal in all situations. Commonly you will want to have elements next to each other as well. This is when floats are utilized.

5.20

In the above example, where a float: left rule has been applied to the class, we can see that the image has been wrapped up tightly and pushed next to the other image. This is the exact nature of a float, it squeezes up an element and forces it into the next bit of available space it can find from the direction specified.

When we state float: left, imagine the element in question starts its journey from the very left position of the parent container and works its way across to the right, finding the first bit of space big enough to contain it. Likewise if we select float: right, the same journey will happen, but from the right-hand side of the page.

Now that we have these images next to each other, we can still make use of all the box model properties we want. Let's add a bit of a margin to the class to space out the images a bit. You can start to see how useful and powerful the box model properties are showing themselves to be already.

5.21

Floats and inline elements

Let's see what using a float on a block-level element next to an inline element does to the flow of a webpage. Take a look at the following example:

```
<div>
    <p>
        <img src="image.jpg" alt="">
        Lorem ipsum dolor sit amet, consectetur adipiscing
        elit, sed do eiusmod tempor incididunt ut labore et
        dolore magna aliqua.
    </p>
</div>
```

5.22

Lorem ipsum dolor sit amet, consectetur adipiscing elit, sed do eiusmod tempor incididunt ut labore et dolore magna aliqua.

This is the default behaviour for the above code. The inline element continues on from the block element and sits next to it, which is great; however, the text seems to continue from the bottom of the image, which isn't the best use of the space available to us.

Now let's add a left float to the image and see how it affects things. Notice how the text wraps tightly around the image where before it rendered on a new line? Well, by applying the float to the image, we can tightly wrap it up and allow the rest of the content to flow around it. Almost like the div is 'floating' in the general flow of the document, right? As you can see, all other content must wrap itself around it as the floated element refuses to move. Once again we can apply some margin and padding to give the image a bit more space to breathe, and now we have something a bit easier to read (Figure 5.23).

```
float: left;
margin: 0px 20px 10px 0px;
```

5.23

Some points to note

Floats will always honour the padding of their parent container. When we float an element, the element will float within the constraints of its parent element (container). This means that if the container has a padding of say 20px, then our left floated image will sit in the far left left-hand corner of this element offset by 20px as we can see in Figure 5.24.

5.24

Floating inline elements

The float property is extremely powerful. We can even specify floats on inline elements, such as the <p> tag. Floating an inline element will force it to behave just like a block element, meaning that it will be wrapped up tightly and put into the next available space.

Sizing

When floating an element, generally you will want to specify a width for the element. By default the element will expand as far as the content inside it needs to, so if the content is text based, it will expand to the entire width of the containing element. Specifying a width of, say, 200px will force the height to expand and will restrict the width of the element to allow us to move it into place, which is the main purpose of floating an element.

Clearing floats

We can use the 'clear' property to force an element to ignore the floats used above it. For example, if I float an image in the top left of a container, then add another element in the HTML, by default the next element will flow around the floated image. This isn't always the desired outcome, however. This is where the clear property comes into play. We can declare the clear property with any of the following values: left, right, both, none.

Let's consider the following example where we have a left and right floated image. You will notice that the right image is slightly longer than the left image, and that the inline paragraph element is flowing nicely around the images.

5.25

Lorem ipsum dolor sit amet, consectetur adipiscing elit, sed do eiusmod tempor inc ididunt ut labore et dolore magna aliqua. Ut enim ad minim veniam, quis nostrud exercitation ullamco laboris nisi ut aliquip ex ea commodo consequat. Duis aute irure dolor in reprehenderit in voluptate velit esse

Let's look at how this example changes when we make use of the clear property on our paragraph tag.

Specifying 'left' will force the new element to break out on to the next available space underneath the bottom of the lowest reaching left floated element above.

```
clear: left;
```

5.26

Lorem ipsum dolor sit amet, consectetur adipiscing elit, sed do eiusmod tempor incididunt ut labore et dolore magna aliqua. Consectetur adipiscing elit, sed do eiusmod tempor incididunt ut labour et dolore magna aliqua.

Similarly, specifying right will look for the lowest hanging right floated element and break out the content to below this.

```
clear: right;
```

27

Lorem ipsum dolor sit amet, consectetur adipiscing elit, sed
do eiusmod tempor incididunt ut labore et dolore magna
aliqua. Consectetur adipiscing elit, sed do eiusmod tempor

And finally, naturally specifying both will clear both left and right
floats forcing the content on to a completely new line underneath
the lowest hanging floated element. Which, in our case, is the image
floated to the right, so the result is the same as 'clear: right' as we
can see below.

28

Lorem ipsum dolor sit amet, consectetur adipiscing elit, sed
do eiusmod tempor incididunt ut labore et dolore magna
aliqua. Consectetur adipiscing elit, sed do eiusmod tempor

Exercise

You can read about floats and clear for an eternity and feel like
you have a good understanding of how they work, but like all
things in web design, until you get out there and experiment

yourself with how it all works together, you will struggle to fully grasp how powerful, useful and also downright frustrating floats can be. So let's walk through a quick example together to see exactly how these properties work in the wild. If you get stuck at any point, just read the section again and give it another shot.

1 Inside your index.html file add a new div and give it an id of 'parent'.

2 Inside the 'parent' element, add five new divs with the following ids: col1, col2, col3, col4, col5 (one per div).

3 Give all of the divs the class of 'col'.

4 In your CSS file, write a new rule for the col class and give it a red background, a width of 50px and a margin of 20px.

5 Now add a rule for the parent div with a width of 500px and a black border.

6 Now give col1 a height of 500px and a left float.

7 Give col2 a height of 400px and a left float.

8 Give col3 a height of 300px and a left float.

9 Give col4 a height of 200px and a right float.

10 Give col5 a height of 100px and a right float.

11 Now add a <p> tag after these divs and give it an id of 'test'.

12 Add some dummy text to the 'test' element, but make sure to put enough in to fill the entire width of your screen.

Note: it is generally best practice to make use of dummy text called 'Lorem ipsum' for testing website designs due to its non-distracting nature. Lorem ipsum can be found with a simple Google search and copying the text from one of the sources. A typical extract looks like this: 'Lorem ipsum dolor sit amet, consectetur adipiscing elit, sed do eiusmod tempor incididunt ut labore et dolore magna aliqua.'

15 Save your files.

5.29

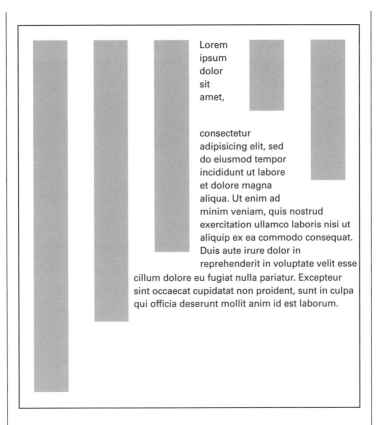

Now stop for a second. What did you expect to see when you opened your floats.html file in Google Chrome? Did you expect to see a nice-looking webpage with text flowing graciously between all of the floated elements? Because that's exactly what we should see. The text should be flowing into every space it can find, just like Figure 5.29.

Let's now experiment with forcing the text to start flowing after certain divs have been cleared:

1   Go back in to your text editor and open your CSS file.

2   Add a CSS rule for test and give it the property of clear: right.

3   Give it a save and have a look at how your page now looks in Google Chrome.

You should now see the following (Figure 5.30):

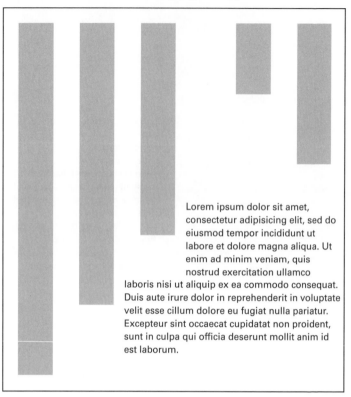

Lorem ipsum dolor sit amet, consectetur adipisicing elit, sed do eiusmod tempor incididunt ut labore et dolore magna aliqua. Ut enim ad minim veniam, quis nostrud exercitation ullamco laboris nisi ut aliquip ex ea commodo consequat. Duis aute irure dolor in reprehenderit in voluptate velit esse cillum dolore eu fugiat nulla pariatur. Excepteur sint occaecat cupidatat non proident, sunt in culpa qui officia deserunt mollit anim id est laborum.

Cool, right? We have now managed to start the text flowing after all of our right floated elements. Now let's change the value of the clear property in our CSS to 'both', which should see the text clearing all of the divs and sitting on a nice new line all on its own (see Figure 5.31).

5.31

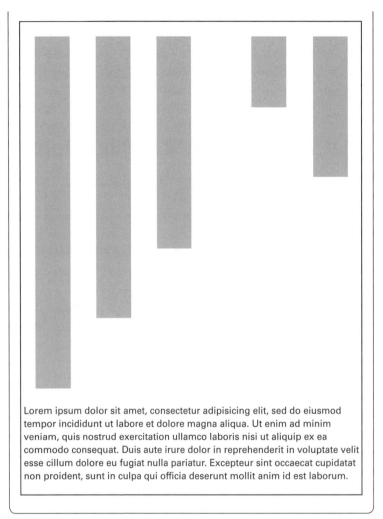

Lorem ipsum dolor sit amet, consectetur adipisicing elit, sed do eiusmod tempor incididunt ut labore et dolore magna aliqua. Ut enim ad minim veniam, quis nostrud exercitation ullamco laboris nisi ut aliquip ex ea commodo consequat. Duis aute irure dolor in reprehenderit in voluptate velit esse cillum dolore eu fugiat nulla pariatur. Excepteur sint occaecat cupidatat non proident, sunt in culpa qui officia deserunt mollit anim id est laborum.

Hopefully this exercise highlights just how useful the clear property can be when working with floated elements. It has allowed us to emulate some of the behaviour of a block-level element on an inline element. The usefulness of this cannot be overstated.

Floats can be extremely helpful, and equally nightmarish at the same time. It will be a while before you are familiar with all of its quirks, but that's half the fun of learning HTML and CSS – working out the kinks and coming out the other side having learned a bit more about how it all fits together. You will be using floats a lot when building your websites, so it's probably a good idea to develop a good patience technique now, ready for your first few attempts at using them in the real world.

What we have learned in this chapter

Now that you're familiar with even more useful CSS concepts, it's time to complete the journey in Chapter 6 with positioning, overlapping and overflow and (of course) more exercises.

06
CSS Part 3

What we will learn in this chapter

In this final CSS chapter, we will complete your teaching in this language with positioning, overlapping and overflow. Let's get started.

Positioning

While floats are a great way of arranging elements around your webpage, they aren't enough to satisfy every demand when positioning elements. This is where the positioning property comes into use. So far we have only looked at elements that sit within the constraints of the flow of the webpage, but sometimes we want a bit more control over our elements. Let's see how making use of the positioning property opens up new possibilities for how we render our elements on our webpage.

The position property

The position property accepts five possible values:

- static;
- relative;
- absolute;
- fixed; and
- inherit.

Each of these values have their own use-cases and quirks, so let's work through them in more detail to further understand how we can make the most of their benefits.

Static

We start with static positioning as this is the default position value for all elements. Static simply means that the elements are positioned how they occur inside the flow of the page. So, just as we have seen already, this simply means that elements will sit naturally depending on whether they are a block or an inline element. Static elements can have floats applied to them to take them outside of the flow, as we have seen in the 'floats' section. Simplistically speaking, static simply means standard.

Relative

Here's where things start to get a bit more interesting. Relative positioning adds the possibility of moving the element around the page while still preserving the space from its initial placement on the document. This sounds complicated, but it's actually very simple.

If we observe a typical div created with the following HTML and CSS code:

```
HTML
<h1>
an <span>example</span> snippet of text
</h1>

CSS
span {
position: relative;
}
```

Which generates the following elements:

an example snippet of text

As you can see, we have applied the value 'relative' to the position property. Now that the element has been assigned this value, we are able to use a set of new properties that we haven't seen before. They are as follows:

- left;
- right;
- top; and
- bottom.

These properties are simple enough to understand and use. They simply allow you to state how much to move the element from the specified direction. So giving the left property a value of '30px' would move the element along 30px from the left. Likewise, giving the top property a value of 30px would move the element down by 30px.

So if we now update our CSS rule to make use of our new positioning properties, like so:

```
<h1>
an <span>example</span> snippet of text
</h1>

CSS
span {
position: relative;
left: 30px;
top: 10px;
}
```

We can see how the element has moved by the specified amount.

an example snippet of text

You can also see that the original space where the text was once positioned is reserved and continues to 'influence' the surrounding content. This is because relative positioned elements still preserve their original space in the document flow.

You might have also noticed how shifting the span element over 30px from the left has resulted in the text overlapping. This is one of the drawbacks of using this positioning style as it can cause overlapping of elements when adjusting the position.

Positioning an element relative is rarely used in this way as its uses are very limited. It's actually at its most useful when paired with a child element with an 'absolute' positioning value. Let's explore this now.

Absolute

Absolute positioned elements are very flexible as they in no way influence the surrounding elements. This is another value that's easier to show than explain. So let's pick up where we left off with the previous example. Let's take the same code and swap out the position value for 'absolute', like so.

```
<h1>
an <span>example</span> snippet of text
</h1>

CSS
span {
position: absolute;
left: 30px;
top: 10px;
}
```

Notice how the element moves again, but closes up the space that was once reserved for it. Absolutely positioned elements exist on their own, having no influence on other elements.

an example: snippet of text

You can imagine how useful this can be. With absolute positioning we are able to take an element and render it exactly where we please on the page. This is hugely useful for content that sits outside of a typical page template. A section of key facts on a website might be an example of content that could make use of absolutely positioning an element.

It doesn't end there, as absolutely positioned elements have one more feature to their makeup that is extremely useful. They are always positioned relative to their closest positioned ancestor. Double Dutch? Allow me to elaborate.

When we give an element any position value that is not 'static' (relative, absolute, fixed) we are 'positioning' this element. This positioned element then becomes the positioned parent to any elements nested inside it. If you so wish, you can then give a position to those child elements, which will then also become the 'positioned ancestor' to any of its children.

Let's see some examples of how this relates to our 'closest positioned ancestor' statement.

First, let's see this in action with the following code snippet:

```
<div id="top-level" class="centered">
  Top Level
  <div id='second-level' class="centered">
    Second Level
    <div id='our-content'> Our content </div>
  </div>
</div>
```

```
CSS
.centered {
width:100%;
margin: 0 auto;
border: 1px solid red;
padding: 20px;
}
#second-level {
position: relative;
}
#our-content {
border: 1px solid blue;
}
```

As you can see, our content sits within its containing div as is expected functionality (see Figure 6.1).

6.1

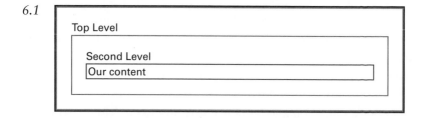

Now let's give our content div an 'absolute' position and specify where it should sit. When using left, right, top and bottom properties with an absolute positioned element, you are specifying how far from the edge of its parent you want the element to be. Let's see this in action, updating our CSS like so:

```
#our-content {
border: 1px solid blue;
position: absolute;
top: 0;
left: 0;
}
```

Now let's see how that changes our page (see Figure 6.2).

6.2

Notice how our content is now taken out of the flow and position 'absolutely' to its parent? Notice how it also ignores all padding inside the box and positions itself relative to its parents' edges? This technique is widely used across the web, and I'm sure you can see why. It's extremely versatile and can help out a lot when defining page layouts.

Now let's see what happens if we remove the position: relative attribute from the second-level div and place the rule over in the top-level div like so:

```
#top-level {
  position: relative;
}
#second-level {
}
```

Now let's see how that changes our page again (see Figure 6.3).

6.3

| Our content |
| Top Level |
| Second Level |

You will notice how the content has now skipped over its direct parent entirely and has positioned itself to the top-level div, even though it exists two levels up from itself in the page hierarchy.

Well, this is because an absolutely positioned element will traverse up the chain to find its closest parent which is 'positioned' and align itself to it. Fantastic, right? I cannot emphasize enough how useful this technique is when it comes to the layout of your webpage.

Now let's take things one step further and remove all the position: relative rules from our CSS. What do you expect to happen in this scenario where no positioned parent can be found?

```
#top-level {
}
#second-level {
}
```

6.4

Was that what you were expecting? As you can see, when no positioned parent can be found, the element gets placed against the body of the webpage. This is a great technique for placing elements outside of the constraints of any other element, and allowing it to sit in isolation. This can be especially useful for building nav bars, buttons and sidebars.

This level of control that we have over our absolutely positioned elements is what makes them such a joy to use in web design. Developers are able to fine-tune exactly where they want an element to sit, regardless of where its parent is on the page. I cannot overstate how useful this is for a developer.

Overlapping

We've seen two examples now, both of which have seen elements overlapping on the page. This is obviously a big issue as it causes a host of usability issues. CSS allows us a way of overcoming this problem by allowing us to 'stack' these elements. By stack, I mean choose the order of how the elements sit on top of one another. We can do this by making use of the z-index property.

z-index is a property that takes a number as its value. The number is its 'importance' in the stack. Let's see an example.

```
<div class="absolute" id="one">One</div>
<div class="absolute" id="two">Two</div>
<div class="absolute" id="three">Three</div>
.absolute {
position: absolute;
background: red;
padding: 10px;
}
```

```
Three
```

As you can see, the divs all stack on top of each other. By default, the top element will be the element positioned last in the HTML code. Let's override this default functionality by assigning a z-index to our first div.

```
#one {
  z-index: 1;
}
```

One

As you can see, our first div is now showing up on the top of the stack. Now let's override this one too by giving our second div a higher z-index value, like so:

```
#one {
z-index: 1;
}
#two {
z-index: 2;
}
```

Two

As you can see, because of the higher value, the second div showed up on top of the pile.

There are no restrictions on what number you use for your rule – it's completely up to you. However, there is actually a max number that browsers will support, which is, very specifically 2147483647. So, you know, try to avoid numbers that high …

Fixed

This one is a lot of fun and once again incredibly useful. Fixed positioning sets the element relative to the viewport.

Viewport

A viewport is the entire browsing window that the user can currently see.

This means that no matter how far down the page the user scrolls, a fixed element will always be visible. It 'sticks' to the viewport and all other content will pass over it either in front or behind as the page scrolls.

Let's see it in action.

```
<div id="fixed">Fixed</div>
#fixed {
position: fixed;
top: 0;
left: 0;
width: 100%;
background: red;
padding: 10px;
}
```

As you can see, the div forces itself to the very top of the page. Fixed elements exist outside the flow of the page and are always relative to the viewport, never any containing divs. This can be quite restrictive at times, as positioning a static item in relation to other elements on the page can be difficult to achieve, but with JavaScript this can be helped (more on JavaScript in the next chapter).

An example of an element that typically uses a fixed position is a nav bar. A navigation bar typically sits on top of all other content at the very top of the page, and does not move regardless of where the user scrolls to on the page. This ensures that the user is able to get to the navigation options at all times. This helps usability of your webpage and is a widely used technique in the modern web landscape.

Exercise

As you have probably concluded by now, the position property is a big deal in web design and it's fundamentally important to have a solid grasp on the various values before moving any further in this book. To solidify our learning, let's put what we have learned into practice. Let's create a website menu system using the techniques outlined above, following these steps:

1 Inside your index.html page, create a new div with an id of 'nav-bar'.

2 Give the nav-bar some CSS rules to make it a fixed position element.

3 Make the element sit at the top of the page and stretch to the full width of the page.

4 Inside the nav-bar include an unordered list (ul) of links.

5 Using the techniques outlined above and in the previous chapters position the links side by side without any bullet icons rendering at all.

6 Save your work and preview in the browser.

Overflow

Overflow refers to content that exists outside of the bounds of an element. If, for instance, we have a div, which we set the height and width of, then add text content to. If the text spans out further than the size of our div, then we need to specify how the browser should handle this situation. By default, the content would spill out from the bottom of the box, which can look untidy. Let's see our options for improving this.

Below, we will look at the example of an overflowing box with no CSS rule in place for overflow, so default values will be used.

```
<div>
Lorem ipsum dolor sit amet, consectetur adipiscing
elit, sed do eiusmod tempor incididunt ut labore et
dolore magna aliqua. Ut enim ad minim veniam, quis
```

```
nostrud exercitation ullamco laboris nisi ut aliquip
ex ea commodo consequat. Duis aute irure dolor in
reprehenderit in voluptate velit esse cillum dolore eu
fugiat nulla pariatur. Excepteur sint occaecat cupidatat
non proident, sunt in culpa qui officia deserunt mollit
anim id est laborum
</div>

div {
 width: 200px;
 height: 100px;
 border: 2px solid black;
}
```

6.5

Lorem ipsum dolor sit amet, consectetur adipiscing elit, sed do eiusmod tempor incididunt ut labore et dolore magna aliqua. Ut enim ad minim veniam, quia nostrud exercitation ullamco laboris nisi ut aliquip ex ea commodo consequat. Duis qute irure dolor in reprehenderit in voluptate velit esse cillum dolore eu fugiat nulla pariatur. Excepteur sint occaecat cupidatat non proident, sunt in culpa qui officia deserunt mollit anim id est laborum

As you can see, the text is spilling out of our box and looking very untidy. Let's see what we can do here.

The available options are as follows:

- Visible. Visible is the default selection. It simply allows the content to overflow and renders the content outside of the element's containing box.

- Hidden. Hidden is as self-explanatory as you would hope it to be – it simply hides the overflowing content. Everything inside the div will be shown, everything outside will be hidden. This is a very useful value, especially when working with overflowing images.

- Scroll. This creates a mini scroll-area. The div will adopt a scrollbar which will allow users to scroll up and down inside the div to see the overflowing content.

- Auto. This value specifies that if the content is overflowing, a scrollbar will be added to allow the user to scroll to see the remaining content. If content is not overflowing, then no scrollbar will be added. This differs from the scroll value as the scroll bar is not always present regardless of whether the content is actually spilling out or not, like it is when 'scroll' is used.

These four options are very useful and powerful and can even be used for non-text content inside the element. Even other divs that are absolutely positioned inside the div will be affected and clipped if overflowing.

Exercise

There will undoubtedly come a time in your future web development career where you will need to make use of this great property, so let's get you practising using it.

1   Open your index.html document back up and create a new div at the top of the page.

2   Give it a width of 600px and a height of 300px.

3   Fill your div with an introductory paragraph explaining a bit about yourself.

4   Decide how you want to handle the overflowing text and assign the appropriate value to the div (feel free to experiment with a few of the different values).

5   Save and preview in the browser.

What we have learned in the CSS section

Well, that was quite a section, right? We just covered the entirety of the fundamentals of CSS. Great job in getting this far. You are well on your way to becoming a fully fledged web designer now. At this point you have mastered enough skills to be able to create your own website using the most fundamental elements of HTML and the most important rules of CSS.

We have seen lists, links, tables, images, divs, headers and even web forms. We have seen how to apply padding, margins, heights, widths, outlines, backgrounds, borders and even understood the mechanics of positioning elements. We really have covered a lot and you have done fantastically well to get this far. Keep up the good work!

We have now built a basic website structure, and explored many different HTML elements and CSS rules, but we have yet to explore interactivity within HTML. Let's address this in the next section where we can now turn our focus to the most challenging part of the book so far, JavaScript. We're going to keep it light and just cover the fundamentals to help you to get started on your journey into learning more JavaScript in your own time and at your own pace.

Part Three
JavaScript

So far in this book we have covered how to define and structure the content of our webpages using HTML and then how to style that content using CSS. Now we turn our focus to how we define the webpage behaviour. This is where JavaScript comes into play.

JavaScript is the language that will add interactivity to your webpages. It is a programming language, the first we have seen in this book and it is also the only programming language that can run in your browser. This is what makes it the de facto standard for adding interactivity to your webpage, as there simply is no alternative. Learning JavaScript is a must for all serious web designers and developers.

So, what exactly can JavaScript do for your webpage? Well, JavaScript can do just about anything from creating alert prompts to appear on your webpage, to changing text dynamically at the click of a button, or even animating elements and a whole lot more.

07
JavaScript Part 1

What we will learn in this chapter

In this chapter, we're going to take a look at how JavaScript is used to dynamically modify our webpage. We'll start with a basic example.

Let's analyse the following code snippet:

```
HTML
<div id="hello-world"></div>
<script>
document.getElementById("hello-world").innerHTML =
"Hello World!";
</script>
```

You are now looking at your first snippet of JavaScript. We won't break down the syntax just yet, but we will analyse what is going on here. You'll notice we have added a set of <script> tags to wrap around our JavaScript. This is the most basic way of getting JavaScript to run on your page. The <script> tag tells the browser that we are trying to execute JavaScript code and to process it as JavaScript. In this example, if you were to save the code as a .html file and open it in the browser, the page would show Hello World! as if the text had been entered into the div all along – however, this isn't the case.

JavaScript runs when you open the webpage, so for a short amount of time the 'hello-world' div would have been completely empty, until the browser reached the JavaScript code, which it executed and carried out its request of placing the Hello World! text into the 'hello-world' div.

This is only a basic example. JavaScript can do a lot more than simply insert text into a div. Let's continue on our journey to master the basics of JavaScript.

Executing JavaScript

As we have seen above, JavaScript runs nicely when entered directly into your webpage. When placing your <script> tag you typically place it either inside the body tag or inside the head tag. It is generally considered best practice to place your script tags at the bottom of the body element as this improves the page loading speed. When the browser hits a snippet of JavaScript, it has to process it, which slows down the display speed of the page. Therefore, if we place our script tags at the bottom, the browser can go through and render all of the elements, then run the scripts at the end. This way the user will see the page render quicker than if the script tags were placed in the middle of the HTML tags.

Using the <script> tags is a nice and easy way of getting your code to execute, but it's not the only way. Using script tags can get quite messy, especially if we have a lot of JavaScript code to run. Your HTML page can end up getting very long and confusing, not to mention difficult to navigate, if you include all of your script directly on the page. Like with CSS, this is where using external files comes into practice. As with CSS we can create a separate file (in this case with a .js file extension), which we can point a reference to and our webpage will then find and include the file for us, just like we do with our external stylesheets.

Scripts are loaded using the following snippet:

```
<script src="script.js"></script>
```

Where you place this script tag will determine where your code is executed just like with placing your <script> tag. Likewise, you should be aiming to place your script reference at the bottom of your body for the best performance possible.

Just like with image files, your path to your script in the reference can be be either an absolute or a relative link.

Syntax

JavaScript is a fantastic programming language, and what's more, it's actually fairly easy to pick up the basics relatively quickly. So let's now take a look at how we structure our JavaScript.

JavaScript statements

A JavaScript statement is comprised of:

- values;
- operators;
- expressions;
- keywords; and
- comments.

Values

JavaScript values are simply pieces of data. Each value, or piece of data, has a type. That type defines the type of content that we are expecting. There are six different basic types for values. They are:

- numbers;
- strings;
- Booleans;
- objects;
- functions; and
- undefined values.

Numbers

As you might have guessed, a value with a 'number' type is a value formed of a numerical value. They are written and displayed as you might expect, as numbers, such as '4231432'.

Strings

Strings are simply snippets of text. It could be a paragraph, a sentence, or even a single character. It is simply a snippet of text of any length.

Boolean

A Boolean is a true/false value. It is usually used for evaluation of a statement. For example, 3<2 would render false, while 3>2 would render true as 3 is a larger number than 2.

Objects, functions, undefined

These will be covered in more detail in the subsequent chapters.

Variables

Variables are what we use to store our data values. They are like buckets of information where we can store and modify the contents as we please. In JavaScript we use the keyword 'var' followed by a keyword and an equals sign to declare a variable, like so:

```
<script>
var x = 100;
var helloWorld = &#x201C;Hello World!;
</script>
```

In this example, the x variable will contain the number 100, while the helloWorld variable will contain the text 'Hello World!'.

Naming variables

When naming things with JavaScript, such as variables, just like with HTML ids and classes, we can't have any spaces in the word. However, when working with programming languages, it is common practice to (instead of using hyphens) replace spaced words with a style of writing known as camelCase. The basic principle of camelCase, is that for each new word, we remove the space and replace the first letter of the new word with a capital letter, except the very first letter of the phrase, which is always lowercase. For example, the phrase 'My New Variable' would become 'myNewVariable'. One of the main reasons we have different 'rules' for naming things between JavaScript and HTML, is to help us quickly decipher the difference between the two when we are working with HTML in JavaScript (more on that later).

Exercise

Let's take a quick breather to try out setting variables ourselves. Head over to your browser and open up the JavaScript developer console. On Google Chrome this can be done by going to: view > developer > JavaScript console
 Then you will see the following pane open up.
 Now carry out the following steps:

- Declare a variable with a name of your choosing and assign it a numerical value of your choice.

- Type the name of your variable back into the console.

- See what happens.

You should see the console repeat your assigned value back to you. If you don't see this, read through the above code again and repeat these steps until you do see your assigned value repeated back to you.

Operators

Now we can start to have some real fun with JavaScript. Let's take a look at operators. Operators are ways of carrying out an 'operation' (or a task) on our data. So, for example, we can use the + operator to add numbers together like so:

```
<script>
var x = 4 + 4;
</script>
```

The value of the x variable here would be 8.

We have already used an operator in the previous exercise. When you assigned the variable, you made use of the assignment operator '='.

Arithmetic operators

There are many different operators available to us. The arithmetic-based operators are as follows:

- + Addition. Adds numbers together.
- - Subtraction. Subtracts numbers from one another.
- Multiplication. Multiplies numbers together.
- / Division. Divides numbers from each other.
- % Modulus. Returns the remainder left after a division. For example, 10 % 3 would be 1 because 3 * 3 gets you to 9, leaving the remainder 1 to get to 10.
- ++ Increment. This will add 1 to your number.
- -- Decrement. This will subtract 1 from your number.

We can combine any number of these together to form an output, like so:

```
// value of x would be 10
var x = 4 * 5 / 2;
```

We can also use parenthesis to help formulate our formula, like so:

```
// value of x would be 2
var x = (4 * 5) / (2 * 10);
```

We can also substitute values for variables and use the same operators. This is where programming can become very useful, with these reusable values. Let's see an example:

```
var x = 4;
var y = 8;
// value of i would be 12
var i = x + y;
```

You can mix and match both variables and numbers in an expression with the same effect, like so:

```
var x = 4;
var y = 8;
// value of i would be 20
var i = x + y + 8;
```

These arithmetic operators are used extensively when programming with JavaScript. Their uses are endless, but in their simplest form they can be used to create a new number from a user's input. Let's imagine for a second that we wanted to create a website where the user could enter their age and find out roughly how many days they had been alive. Let's work through how this would be possible with JavaScript below:

Exercise

Let's put this into practice and get you thinking like a programmer. I want you to do the following:

- Open up the developer console.
- Declare a variable called 'daysInAYear' and set it to the number 365.
- Declare another variable called 'myAge' and set it to your age in years (eg, 23).
- Now declare another variable called 'daysAlive' and set it to daysInAYear multiplied by 'myAge'.
- Now output this variable back to the console and note the value – the number should equal roughly the total number of days you have been alive.

Now, obviously this isn't entirely accurate as it doesn't factor in the day and month of your birth, however you can see how useful JavaScript can be for us when creating these types of dynamic operators.

Assignment operators

We have already seen the = assignment operator in the previous section when declaring our variables, but there are many more that can save you a significant amount of time when defining variables. Let's see the list:

- =

  This is the most basic operator, it simply means assign this data to this variable.

- +=

  This operator assigns a value to a variable and at the same time adds it to its own value. This one makes more sense in practice. Let's see an example:

```
var x = 4;
var x += 8;
// value of x would be 12
```

- -=

  Similar to the previous example, this one subtracts the assigned value from its own value.

- *=

  You can probably guess this one too – it multiplies the assigned value with itself.

- /=

  Once again, similar to above, this one will divide the assigned value with itself.

- %=

  This one is a bit more difficult to work your head around, but operates on the same principles as before. This will perform the modulus operation on the assigned value against itself.

Using these assignment operators can save a lot of time. Compare the following statements:

```
var x = 4;
x = x + 8;
// value of x would be 12

var x = 4;
x += 8;
// value of x would be 12
```

Both produce the same output, but the first does it in far fewer characters of code. This is important when programming as we are always looking for the most succinct way of achieving our desired output. This way our codebase is smaller and easier to read and maintain.

Looking at the above example, you might have noticed that we omitted the 'var' keyword when we 'reassigned' the variables – this is because the 'var' keyword is only used when declaring the variable the first time. Once the variable has been declared, we simply reference the variable using this name.

String operators

String operators are nice and simple as we only have a small number of operators, and they are both used for concatenation of strings. Let's see how they work.

Concatenation

The process of joining one or more pieces of data together.

First we have the + operators again; however, when in the context of using it with a string, instead of adding numbers together, JavaScript will combine the strings together like so:

```
var x = "Hello";
var y = "World!";
var i = x + y;
// value of i would be Hello World!
```

Looking at the above example, you might be wondering how we would go about adding a space between the words? Have a go yourself in your console and see if you can work out a good way of achieving this.

Have you had a go yet? Great, let's look at the solution. We simply use a string containing a space. We can do this inside one of the variables, like so:

```
var x = "Hello";
var y = "World!";
var i = x + y;
// value of i would be Hello World!
```

As you can see, we have added a trailing space after hello, which forces the space in the final output; however, this can be an issue if we want to ever use the string again in our code but don't need the space (code reuse is a top priority when programming), therefore a better and more commonly used approach is to concatenate a space inside your output, like so:

```
var x = "Hello";
var y = "World!";
var i = x + " " + y;
// value of i would be Hello World!
```

Notice how you can combine multiple strings in one statement. You can also add strings directly in the declaration without having to define it as a separate variable.

Lastly, with strings you can also make use of the += operator to concatenate multiple strings in a less verbose manner, like this:

```
var x = "Hello";
var y = "World!";
var y += x;
```

You can also combine numbers and strings using the + operator with great effect. It doesn't perform a calculation on the number, but merely turns the number into a string and joins the two strings together. Let's take a closer look:

```
var x = "Hello";
var y = 5;
y += x;
// value of y is 'Hello5'
```

When combining a string with a number the output will always be a string. In the above example, y is now a string.

Other operators

There are many more operators available to us in JavaScript, which we will come across in subsequent chapters where they are more relevant, but for now, these are the main operators we are going to be working with. Let's ensure we have a firm grasp of how they all work so far.

Operators are used everywhere in JavaScript. They form the basics of assigning and manipulating variables to our requirements. They afford us full control over how we want to manipulate our data and allow us to perform very powerful operations. They are used in conjunction with the majority of other concepts you will learn in this book, so it's very important you fully understand how they function and 'operate'.

Exercise

Once again, this exercise will take place in the developer console and will test your knowledge of the above concepts. These concepts form the core of JavaScript and it's extremely important you have a firm grasp on how they work. If you are unable to complete this exercise with the expected output, please revisit the above content and attempt it again. It's important that you don't try to progress further without understanding these basic operators:

1 Open up the developer console.

2 Create a variable and assign it a string with the following text 'my age is'.

3 Now create a new variable and give it a number corresponding to your age.

4 Now concatenate the second variable to the first, ensuring legibility. Experiment with adding a colon between the text and the number.

5 Now output this variable back to the console.

6 Ensure it renders like so: 'My age is: 00' where 00 is your inputted age.

Functions

Functions are the building blocks of a piece of JavaScript code. They are reusable snippets of code that perform an action (or task). Functions are run (executed) when something 'invokes' or 'calls' it. This might sound complicated, but once you see a few examples it will all become clearer. Let's kick off with a nice and easy function for us to analyse:

```
function exampleFunction(par1, par2) {
   return par1 + par2;      // The function returns the product
          of p1 and p2
}
```

As you can see above, a function in JavaScript is defined by using the 'function' keyword. After the function keyword you will specify the name of your function. You can call this whatever you like, but it cannot contain spaces, so camelCase is the standard method for defining function names, just like with variables.

Inside the parenthesis you specify your 'parameters' separated by commas. You can include as many as you like or even none at all. The code to be executed by the function is contained within the curly braces.

The return statement inside the curly braces is the data that we want to return from the function. As soon as the code reaches a return statement, the function execution is stopped and the return value is returned.

The parameters in a function are effectively just simple variables – they can be a string, a number, a Boolean or any other value type. Their actual values are 'passed in' when the function is invoked later on in the code. It's important to note that the parameters will always be local to the function. This also means that any variables defined within the function will only exist inside the function.

We can run this function in the following way:

```
var x = exampleFunction(1, 4);
```

In the above snippet, we are setting the value of x to the returned value of the 'exampleFunction'; we pass the function the values 1 and 4, these then become par1 and par2 when inside the function as they are passed through from the parenthesis through to the code inside the curly braces. In this example, the code then adds the two values together and returns the result. After this line of code is run, the variable x will be equal to 5.

Functions are completely reusable. We can define it once and use it as many times as we like, passing in different values each time to suit our needs. This is the magic of programming – you can write a function just one time and use it throughout your entire website to speed up your development time and keep things consistent.

Exercise

It's important you have a solid understanding of how functions work, so let's put your skills of observation to the test and get you writing your own function. Once again, we are going to carry out this exercise inside the Google Chrome JavaScript console.

1 Open up the developer console.

2 Define a function that takes in at least two parameters (hold shift while pressing enter to ensure you are able to write the function over multiple lines without executing the function before you have finished declaring it).

3 Have the function return a value using any of the operators covered in the previous section.

4 Now call the function with any values you choose.

5 Ensure you get the expected response before moving on to the next section.

Outputting information

One of the main functions of JavaScript is to present information to your users in ways that are not possible with pure CSS and HTML. Here are some of the ways that JavaScript can output information:

- Outputting to an element. Displaying text inside an element, as we saw in the above example.

- Writing to the HTML output. This simply outputs the text onto the webpage wherever the script was executed.

- Outputting to an alert box. This will output your text into a popup alert box, which will force an action from your user to close it.

- Writing to the 'console' in your browser. This is used for debugging and testing of your code.

Let's look into these four different ways of presenting information in JavaScript in more detail.

Outputting to an element

Let's look again at our earlier example which introduced us to JavaScript and illustrated this technique of outputting text using the inner HTML method.

```
HTML
<div id="hello-world"></div>
<script>
  document.getElementById("hello-world").innerHTML =
  "Hello World!";
</script>
```

As you can see, inside the parentheses and double quotes is the name of the element we are targeting as the destination for the new text, then the text in double quotes after the = sign is our desired new text snippet. The statement is then 'terminated' or 'executed' with a semi-colon.

This is an example of the standard way to output text to an element using the JavaScript method document.getElementById(id).

Writing to the HTML output

We can make use of the document.write method to output data directly to the webpage document. Like so:

```
HTML
<div id="hello-world">Hello World</div>
<script>
document.write("Test");
</script>
```

This will output the text 'Test' in plain text on the page. This is mainly only ever used for testing purposes. It's important to note that using document.write after a page has loaded will replace all of the existing HTML content that had rendered.

Outputting to an alert box

We can use the window.alert() method to output to an alert box. An alert box is the prompt that you see on a website that often prompts for action. Below is an example of a common prompt you might see when browsing the web.

The code snippet for this is as follows:

```
<script>
window.alert('Hello world!');
</script>
```

This snippet of code would automatically run on page load, so the prompt would appear right away.

Writing to console

The console is a powerful debugging tool built into all modern browsers. It is a tool to display informative messages about your website. You can push a message to the log by making use of the console.log() method.

Let's see how it works:

```
<script>
console.log('Hello world!');
</script>
```

This snippet will output the text 'Hello world!' to the log and will only be seen if you manually look into the webpage console.

Statements

So far we have seen many lines of JavaScript code just like this:

```
console.log('Hello world!');
```

Each of these snippets of code that perform an action are called statements. When programming with JavaScript we make use of many statements in a specified order, like a recipe, in order to perform a designated set of actions, in a very specific sequence, in order for us to achieve our desired output. Consider the following code:

```
var x = 'Hello world';
console.log(x);
```

When this code is processed in the browser, the JavaScript engine will execute the statements in the exact order that it sees them. So in this case, it will assign the string 'Hello world' to the variable x, then log that variable to the console. The order here is important. If we were to switch the order that the statements run, like so:

```
console.log(x);
var x = 'Hello world';
```

We would get an error and our code would not execute correctly. The reason for this error is simple, right? x isn't defined at the point at which we ask the browser to log the variable x. So x returns 'undefined'.

To recap, JavaScript statements are executed in the exact order that they are written, and variables must always be defined before use. Simple stuff, but critically important to understand.

Semi-colons

You might have noticed semi-colons at the end of each statement we have written so far and wondered what part they play in the statement. A semi-colon in JavaScript terminates a statement. It marks the end of the statement and instructs the next statement to run. Interestingly, semi-colons aren't actually required at all as a method of executing a statement. It's totally fine to leave a semi-colon off the end of a statement, and the statement will still execute the same; however, it is strongly recommended to make use of semi-colons as it helps to clearly define each statement, and also allows you to specify multiple statements on a single line, like so:

```
var x = 'Hello world'; console.log(x);
```

The above code is identical to:

```
var x = 'Hello world'
console.log(x)
```

which is also identical to:

```
var x = 'Hello world';
console.log(x);
```

All of these blocks of code will be handled in the exact same way by the JavaScript engine; however, the recommended method would always be to format your code as such:

```
var x = 'Hello world';
console.log(x);
```

Writing each statement on a new line, and ending it with a semi-colon, increases readability of your code, which is important when you come back to review your code in the future and also for any other programmers who might need to alter your code at some point in the future. Always aim to write code that is well structured as it makes your life a lot easier further down the road.

Other best practices

While on the topic of best practices, it is also a good idea to pad your statements out with white space where possible, specifically around operators. White space is ignored in JavaScript, so it's always a good idea to make use of white space as a means of writing more readable code. Here is an example of how using white space around operators helps to increase readability:
Before

```
var y="Hello";
var x=y+' World!';
```

After

```
var y = "Hello";
var x = y + ' World!';
```

As you can see, we have added spaces around the '=' and '+'. As a result, the code is much more readable and maintainable. This is best practice, which you should strive towards when writing your JavaScript code.

Another best practice that developers tend to abide by is capping line lengths. Programmers tend to cut their lines off at 80 characters for increased readability. When breaking a statement, it's usually best to break it at an operator (=, –, =, etc).

One of the final best practices we will discuss for formatting statements is around code blocks. Typically, developers will group together statements that are intended to be run together to achieve a certain action into a function that can be run at will. Let's see an example of this in action:

After

```
function helloWorld() {
var y = "Hello";
var x = y + ' World!';
console.log(x);
}
```

These statements can then be run easily in one simple command.

```
helloWorld();
```

The last best practice we will look at is around commenting your code. Comments are a key part of a programmer's role. Comments in your JavaScript are snippets of text where a developer will explain a part of the code in plain English. Comments are wrapped in tags to highlight them as non-executable. Comments are never executed by the JavaScript engine; it simply skips right past them as if they don't exist.

There are many ways to specify and format a comment. Let's look first at line comments.

A line comment is signified by a prefixing //. Any text after the // and before the end of the line, will be treated as a comment. There are two ways we can make use of this.

Developers can describe a statement on the line directly above the statement like so:

```
<script>
// Show a popup that says 'Hello world!'
window.alert('Hello world!');
</script>
```

As you can see, the descriptive line is directly above the statement it is explaining. You can describe the statement in any way you choose and can use any special characters of your choosing. It will all be treated as text regardless of any special syntax you use.

If you have a statement that is particularly short, for example defining a variable, it can be useful to add the comment directly after the statement. Remember that anything after the // will be treated as a comment until the end of the line.

```
var y = "Hello"; // Declare a variable with the string
  'Hello'
var x = y + ' World!'; // Join the variable y with the
  string World!'
console.log(x); // Log the variable x to the console
```

As you can see, this is a much cleaner and clearer way to document your code – just try to make sure the entire line (statement and comment) are below the 80-character best practice for line lengths.

Block comments

Sometimes it's not beneficial to comment on each individual line of a function if the statement itself is fairly self-explanatory. In this situation it is often better to write a comment about the entire function instead. In these cases, we can make use of block comments. Block comments are started with /* and ended with */. Any text between the two tags is declared as a comment and can span over multiple lines. Let's see an example of how we can make use of block comments in our code:

```
/*
This function declares a variable with the "Hello"
   string, then joins it with "World!"
Then the entire variable is logged to the console
*/
function helloWorld() {
var y = "Hello";
var x = y + ' World!';
console.log(x);
}
```

This approach helps us to write code that is easy to read and interpret, and which can be understood by any new developer who might be looking over your code in the future.

Using comments for testing purposes

Comments can be a great way to test and debug your code. When you are writing your code and facing a problem with its execution, it is sometimes useful to help isolate the problem by 'removing' a line of code to see where your script 'breaks'. 'Commenting out' a single line of code is a great way to do this, rather than removing it entirely. Simply add a // in front of the potentially problematic statement, and instantly it becomes a comment, and therefore does not execute. Remember you can also comment out entire blocks of code using block comments. Let's see some examples of how this might work:

```
var i = "Hello world;
var y = "Hello";
var x = y + ' World!';
console.log(x);
```

In the above example, the first statement – var i = "Hello world; – is missing a closing speech mark, and would break the execution of the entire script. That is to say that when the browser reaches that part of the JavaScript file, it would stop executing, so any subsequent lines of code would not be executed or even read. To fix our code again we could simply comment out the line and our code would execute again, like so:

```
// var i = "Hello world;
var y = "Hello";
var x = y + ' World!';
console.log(x);
```

Now when the browser reaches the broken line of code, it will skip right past it like it doesn't exist, and the rest of our code will execute without any issues.

Commenting your code is an extremely important part of programming. It assists both yourself and other developers in understanding your code when you come to review it in the future. Try to get into the good habit of documenting your code as much as possible.

What we have learned in this chapter

We have covered a lot of ground in this first look at Javascript, from how to execute it, its syntax and best practice, to core concepts such as variables, operators, functions and more. In the next chapter, we will continue our crucial deep dive into this web design language.

08
JavaScript Part 2

What we will learn in this chapter

In Part 2 of our JavaScript section, we will be covering data types, strings and, one of the most important and challenging concepts of JavaScript, objects.

Data types

So far on our journey into the world of JavaScript, we have created many variables and assigned them different values. We have assigned them some snippets of text, such as in our 'Hello World!' examples. We have also assigned them numbers, like in our function examples. Each of these different types of information that we assign to a variable is called a 'data type'. So far we have seen strings (text, such as 'Hello World') and numbers. Let's quickly see examples of these again to refresh our understanding:

```
var x = "Hello"; // Assigning a string
var y = 12; // Assigning a number
```

Data types play a very important part in programming and understanding them is a fundamental part of your learning of JavaScript and its concepts. JavaScript handles the assigning of data types for you when you declare your variables. It will detect the data type you have assigned, based on your syntax. You do not have to specifically state which type of data your variable holds, like you might do in a different programming language.

It's important to understand both the benefits and limitations of each data type, to help you to understand what you can do with each. So let's first understand just why data types are so important.

Consider the following snippet of code:

```javascript
var x = "Hello"; // Assigning a string
var y = 12; // Assigning a number
var i = x + y;
console.log(i);
```

Now pause for a second and think about this snippet of code. What do you think will happen when we try to run this code? Will it break the code and produce an error message? Or will it try to output something in the console and fail there?

Give it a go and see what happens for yourself.

If you did go ahead and run the above code in your console to see what would happen, you were probably surprised by the result. JavaScript simply joins them together.

8.1

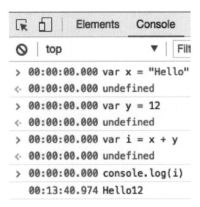

Remember earlier when I said JavaScript detects data types automatically? Well, this is an example of that in action. When we first declare our variables we assign the text 'Hello' to the variable x and the number 12 to the variable y. At this stage variable x contains a string, and variable y contains a number. Then the next line of code sees us attempt to add the variables together. The JavaScript engine sees this, and detects that it's not possible to add a number to a bit of text, so the developer must want to join the variables together instead. In this case the number is not to be treated as a number, but rather another piece of text to join together with the 'Hello' variable. JavaScript then temporarily switches the data type over to a string and joins them together in the new variable. (Don't worry, the initial variable x is still a number after this happens, though.)

Therefore, the output of the code is 'Hello12'.

JavaScript simply evaluates the statement and decides the best way to handle the data types. The evaluation process happens from left to right, meaning as the JavaScript engine makes its way across the line of code, it is constantly evaluating how to handle the expression.

Let's see some examples of how this happens.

Open up Google Chrome and head over to the developer console again. Click the console tab and check out what happens when you enter these statements:

```
var x = 14 + 6 + "Hello World";
console.log(x)
```

What would you expect to happen here? You probably expected the output to be '146Hello World', right? While it might seem like that is what would happen, remember that JavaScript evaluates statements from left to right. When JavaScript sees the 14 after the =, it decides it is looking at a number – because it is – next it sees the 6 (once again a number) so it adds them together. Then it sees the 'Hello World' text, which is undoubtedly a string. It can't add a number to a string, so it just joins them together. Makes sense, right? JavaScript's understanding of the context of the expression grows as it reads the statement from the left, over to the right.

Now let's flip the statements and see what happens:

```
var x = "Hello World" + 14 + 6;
console.log(x)
```

What do you expect to see now that we know how JavaScript evaluates expressions? If you've been paying attention, you will have guessed that the output would be 'Hello World146' and you would be absolutely right. Let's step through it again. JavaScript sees the 'Hello World' and decides it is a string, then it sees the number 14, decides it can't add a string and a number together, so it must join them instead, at which point we have the string 'Hello World14'; then it encounters the final part of the expression, 6, at which point JavaScript understands that it can't add together the string 'Hello World14' with 6, so it must also join them together. Resulting in an output of 'Hello World146'.

In JavaScript data types are dynamic. This means that we can swap out variables to contain different data types at will. If we have a variable that contains a number, we can very easily convert that to a string and vice versa. This is incredibly useful because it means we are never restricted to what we can assign to our variables, even if they have already been declared. The following example highlights this benefit.

```
var x; // variable x is undefined
x = "Hello World"; // variable x is now a string
x = 12; // variable x is now a number
x = x + "Hello World"; // variable x is now a string
again
```

We can pass around variables and reassign them at will to any data type we so choose, without ever having to actually specify which data type we are using. This is a huge benefit to the way JavaScript handles data types.

Knowing the data type of your variable is very important, as each data type allows us to perform different, data type-specific operations on the variable. Let's look at some examples of how different data types allow us to perform different actions.

Numbers

Variables of the 'number' data type are declared by setting the variable to an integer without any quotes around it, like so:

```
var x = 12; // Data type is a number
```

The lack of quotes is extremely important; it's how we tell JavaScript to treat the variable as a number and not a string. Simply wrapping quotes around a number, like so:

```
var x = "12"; // Data type is a string
```

We will render the number as a string, and it will therefore be treated as text, which means we lose the actions we can perform on a variable with a data type of number.

Declaring numbers is very easy; we can specify any number we like of any size. We can even use decimal points like so:

```
var x = 12.55;
```

The main benefit of ensuring our variable is of the number data type, is that we can perform arithmetic operations on the variable as we have seen before. Let's quickly recap with an example of performing some basic arithmetic on a variable:

```
var x = 12 + 14; // Variable x is equal to 26
```

When performing arithmetic, we are able to make use of parenthesis to break up and formulate our statement, like so:

```
var x = (2 + 4) * (2 + 8); // Variable x is equal to 60
```

Using parenthesis can be extremely useful in ensuring JavaScript performs the arithmetic inside the parenthesis before carrying out the query as a whole.

Consider the difference between the following two statements, one with parentheses and one without:

```
var x = (2 + 4) * (2 + 8); // Variable x is equal to 60
var y = 2 + 4 * 2 + 8; // Variable x is equal to 18
```

Performing these actions on a variable is only possible when the variable has the data type of a number. It's not possible to perform these actions on a string, and trying to do so will result in an interesting result.

Let's analyse the following scenario:

```
var x = "12"; // Variable is a string
var y = x * 4;
```

What do you think the assigned value of variable y will be? Undefined? Not quite. The variable gets assigned a special, reserved word in JavaScript. It gets assigned to 'NaN', which is an abbreviation of 'not a number'. When a variable is rendered 'NaN', you lose the ability to perform any arithmetic operations on the variable. The variable is effectively useless at this stage until you redefine it.

You can check whether a value is a number or not by using one of the built-in 'global functions' of JavaScript, called 'isNaN()'. This function will accept a parameter and return either true or false depending if the parameter is a number or not. This probably sounds a bit more confusing than it actually is, so let's see this in action:

```
var x = 12 * "text";
isNaN(x); // Function returns 'true'
```

As you can see above, we have attempted to multiply a number with a string, which is obviously not possible, so it gets set to 'NaN', and, as such, when we pass the variable to the isNaN function, the function checks if the variable is set to NaN, and when it realizes that it is set to NaN, it returns true.

Strings

As we have seen already in this book, strings are the data type used for storing text. Nice and simple, right? Before we dig into what we are able to do without strings, let's take another look at how we define a string.

```
var name = "John" // String of text "John"
```

We simply wrap our text in quotation marks, and we have a string. What if you accidentally use single quotes instead of double quotes? No problem, that will work too. In fact, the two are completely interchangeable. You can create a string with either single or double quotes, like so:

```
var name = "John" // String of text "John"
var name = 'John' // String of text "John"
```

Both of the above variables are completely identical. Now, at this stage you might be wondering why we are able to use either. I mean, why not just standardize it to single or double quotes and leave it at that? Well, let me answer that question with another question: how do you think you might include a quotation inside your string? Imagine you are creating a variable that includes a quote – how would you do that?

Try this:

```
var name = "John said "Hi there developers" and waved";
```

What do you think would happen if we tried to execute this statement? Give it a go and find out for yourself. Head over to your Google Chrome browser, enter the code above and see what happens.

Did you get a nice big error message about unexpected characters? Of course you did – that's because JavaScript doesn't know where your string ends. To JavaScript, it sees you are trying to assign a variable called 'name' with the value 'John said' then it sees some 'random' text 'Hi there developers'. However, JavaScript doesn't know that this is still part of your string as it saw a closing quotation mark, so assumed your string was finished. It doesn't know how to handle 'Hi there developers', so it informs you that it has encountered an unexpected character.

Hopefully you can see why JavaScript would get confused by this statement. How can it know the difference between your quote and the ending of your string? Well, this is why it's so useful to be able to assign strings with both single and double quotes. In JavaScript you can include quotes inside the string as long as they don't match the enclosing quotes, so if you use double quotes on the outside, you must use single quotes on the inside, and vice versa. Let's see some examples to illustrate this better:

```
var name = "John said 'Hi there developers' and waved";
var name = 'John said "Hi there developers" and waved';
```

Both of the above variables are completely valid, but they are slightly different. The first variable stores your quote of 'Hi there developers' in single quotes, while the second stores it in double quotes. This is a point for consideration when declaring your variables. If you need to use double quotes on the inside, you must make sure you use single quotes on the outside. It is not possible to use both, however.

Moving on, let's imagine for a second that we wanted to store a string with the following text 'John said "Hello, it's great to meet you"'. How do you think you might do that?

Give it a go yourself and see if you can figure it out.

Did you work it out? Or did you run into an error message? The tricky part here is that we are trying to create a variable with a string that contains both a single and a double quote inside it, and

that's not possible to do at the same time. A solution to this problem that you might have come to is actually quite straightforward,
but it does require some creative thinking (something that you will
need to get used to if you want to be a programmer!). Let's see the
solution below:

```
var name = 'John said "Hello,' + "it's " + 'great to
meet you"';
```

How you split up the phrase is completely up to you, just as long
as you split up the string into sections depending on whether you
need to store a single or double quote on the inside. Hopefully this
makes sense to you. If not, it's important that you grasp this concept before moving forward. Make sure you are trying out these
examples for yourself in your browser – it will make all the difference with helping you to understand this fully.

Now, while the above code would work just fine, and is a good
exercise for us to go through to understand the problem better,
there is a much simpler way of achieving the same result.

When defining a string, we have a special character available to
us that we can use to help with this exact problem. It's called the
escape character, and is simply denoted with a backslash (\).

Any character immediately after a backslash will be 'escaped'
and turned into part of the string, regardless of its wider meaning.
This means that instead of chopping up a string to contain a quote
inside our text, we can simply write this:

```
var name = "John said \"Hello, it\'s great to meet
you\"";
```

And the output will be exactly the same. The backslash is ignored
and the immediately succeeding character is turned into a string
character. Handy, right? I know what you're probably thinking
right now: 'But what about if I want to use a backslash itself in my

string? How is that possible if backslashes are escaped?' Well, the answer is actually very simple – just do a double backslash, like so:

```
var x = "This is how you output a backslash (\\) in your
string";
```

String methods

Strings are really useful data types. Once we assign a string variable, we are able to manipulate and use that variable in a number of extremely useful ways. String methods are built-in 'helpers' that carry out operations on your string. We are also given many properties on our string. A property is a value, or piece of data that gets created and assigned to our string every time we create one. Let's look at a few of the most useful methods and properties of the string data type now.

string.length

One of the most useful properties that gets assigned to our strings when we create them is the .length property. Before we discuss it in more detail, let's first see how we use it:

```
var x = "This is a string";
var y = x.length
```

You are looking at a new style of syntax that we haven't seen yet on our journey. Let's break down what's happening here. First we create our variable x and assign it a string, then we create another variable, which contains x.length.

What we are doing here is pulling in our variable, then picking off the property 'length' from our variable. Remember how I said whenever we create a string, that string gets assigned some properties? Well, one of those properties is length. Length is simply a property that contains the number of characters in the string. Simple enough, right?

So all we are really doing here is saying 'Can I have the length of the x variable'. We don't care in any way about the actual string itself, the text isn't important to us, we just want to know the length.

Quick side question here, what do you think the value of y is now? If we console.log the variable y, what do you think we would see? Let's take a look together.

```
var x = "This is a string";
var y = x.length // value is 16
console.log(y); // logs 16 to the console
```

Interestingly our variable y is now a number, the number 16. We have created a new variable of the type number, from our variable which is a string. Cool, right?

Congratulations, you have just seen your first property. These will play a big part in our understanding later on in this chapter, so feel free to sit with this concept for a bit to ensure you fully understand exactly what is happening here.

When you're ready to move on, let's take a look at our first method...

search()

The search method is a very useful 'helper' that we can make use of for searching through a string to find a search term. It literally searches the string to find your result. Now you might have noticed that there are parentheses on the end of the word 'search' – a bit like the functions we saw earlier in this chapter. A method is still a property, just like the .length property we just looked at; however, a method is a property that contains a function, rather than a snippet of information.

When we declare a string variable, we assign it to a piece of text, then behind the scenes, JavaScript also assigns a set of properties and methods (remember, methods are actually properties themselves) to our string that we can use at will.

With this in mind, how do you think we might use the search method? Very similarly to our .length property, with a slight twist on things. Let's see an example:

```
var x = "This is a string";
var pos = x.search("string");
```

Take a look at the above code. It's all so familiar, yet so new. You can see many of the principles we have discussed previously, and now we are just bringing them all together. You can see the variable.property syntax that we just saw when looking at .length; you can also see the parenthesis and parameter that we saw when we looked at functions. This is because .search() is just a property containing a function that was added to our string when we created it. This function is a pre-defined function that has been written for us, and it is written in a way that allows us to provide a parameter of our search term, and it will then 'return' information about where that search term is inside of the string.

So in the above example, the variable 'pos' will be assigned the number 10. It will be assigned 10 because the word string can be found at the tenth character into the string. How easy and useful is that? Now, let's look at another useful string method:

.slice()

The .slice method is responsible for chopping up our string into a chunk that we specify. This method accepts unto two parameters, a starting position and an ending position. This one is easier to show than to explain, so let's jump right in with an example:

```
var x = "This is a long string";
var slicedText = x.slice(10, 14);
```

Looking at the above example, we can see that we have provided the slice method with the parameters 10 and 14. Have a think about what you expect to happen here for a second before reading on.

Thought about it? Okay, let's break this down. When we give the first parameter of 10, we are saying 'start cutting the string at the 10th character', which in this case is at the start of the word 'long', then our second parameter of 14 is saying, 'now finish cutting out the word at the 14th character'. Which then gives us the word 'long', which is what the variable slicedText will be assigned to. Simple enough, right?

As with most of the concepts in this book, there's a bit more to it than that. The parameters also accept negative values. Now this isn't as confusing as it sounds. When you specify a negative value, it will count to that value from the end of the string instead of the start, so –5 would be the fifth character from the end of the string. Let's see this in action:

```
var x = "This is a long string";
var slicedText = x.slice(-11, -7);
```

In the above example, the slicedText variable is once again set to 'long' – the same output, just achieved in a different way.

Lastly, it's important to note that the second parameter is completely optional. You can leave it off if you wish and just specify one parameter like so:

```
var x = "This is a long string";
var slicedText = x.slice(10);
```

What do you think will happen in the above snippet of code? Your first guess would probably be that it will just trim the tenth character only, so 'slicedText' will be set to 'l'. While this is a very good and logical guess, in actuality, it simply starts trimming at the tenth character, but then finishes trimming at the very end of the string, regardless of its length. So the slicedText variable will actually be assigned to 'long string'.

You can also use negative values here; you could very easily write this code:

```
var x = "This is a long string";
var slicedText = x.slice(-11);
```

and achieve the exact same output of 'long string'.

substr()

A method that is very similar to the slice method, but its usage differs slightly, is the subset method. The substr method operates in a very similar way: the first parameter is our starting position, just like with slice; however, the second parameter isn't the ending position, but actually the length of the extracted segment. This allows us to specify how many characters we would like to 'cut out' of our string. Let's see it in action:

```
var x = "This is a long string";
var slicedText = x.substr(10, 4);
```

The value of slicedText here, again, is 'long'. As you can see, instead of specifying the final character of the slice's position, we specify 4, which is the length of the word we would like to cut out. This is particularly useful when combined with the .length property, which will allow us to cut out the word without having to know the ending position of the character. Let's see if you can work out how to do this on your own in the following short exercise:

Exercise

- Open up Google Chrome and head over to your inspector tools.
- Now I want you to create a string variable named 'text' containing any text of your choosing.
- Now create a new variable named 'startPos', which contains the result of a search for a term inside your 'text' variable (make sure that the search term does exist inside your string).

- Now create another variable named 'endPos', which contains the value of the length of your text variable (make sure you use the property here and do not hardcode the value yourself).

- Then create one last variable and assign it the result of a substr of your 'text' variable, use the 'startPos' and 'length' variables as your parameters. This should give you a final variable equal to your initial search term.

- Finally, check your code is working by logging your final variable to the console.

Answer

If you managed to get the desired output, well done. You have successfully merged some of the key concepts of programming that we have learned so far into one exercise. Fantastic work. If you didn't get there, that's no problem; these are all new concepts and it's completely understandable to be a bit overwhelmed at this stage. If you are feeling that way, I encourage you to go back, revisit this chapter again from the start, and just brush up on the topics covered and attempt this again. It's important for your own learning and understanding that you are putting into practice what we are learning. If you really can't get this working on your own, then feel free to check out the solution below; but I do encourage all readers to attempt to get there on their own, as you can learn a lot about programming from your mistakes, and it's important to start to get into the mindset of debugging code and trying to work out where you went wrong.

Solution

```
var text = "This is a long string";
var startPos = x.search("long");
var length = x.length;
var slicedText = x.substr(startPos, length);
console.log(slicedText);
```

Other string methods

There are many other string methods that we can make use of in our code. For example:

- replace() – for replacing a value in a string with another value.
- toUpperCase() – for converting a string into entirely uppercase.
- toLowerCase() – for converting a string into entirely lowercase.

We will be making use of some of these functions in the next section of the book, but for now let's move on to take a look at one of the most fundamental aspects of any programming language: objects.

Objects

In JavaScript, objects are everywhere. Pretty much everything in JavaScript is an object. Strings can be objects, numbers can be objects, functions are objects, values are objects, dates are objects, objects are objects. So by now you've probably got the message. Objects are everywhere in JavaScript. So, the obvious question is, what's an object? Well, in programming, objects can be compared directly with an object in real life. Let's take the example of an animal. An animal has properties, right? Like its name, its colour, its size, its weight, its breed or its age. An animal also has methods: an animal can talk, it can sit, it can roll over, it can eat and sleep. Well, you can define an object in JavaScript that represents this exact same idea. Objects simply contain data about a 'thing'. Objects are simply variables that contain more than one piece of information. Ever used a website that you have your own profile on? Which contains your email address, password, address, etc? Well, it's extremely likely that that information will be joined together into an object in the website's JavaScript code. Objects should contain all of the relevant information about one thing. Now, enough explaining. Let's see some code and step through it:

```
var animal = {
name: "Buster",
age: 6,
type: "Husky",
colour: "blue",
speak: function() {
console.log("Woof");
}
}
```

Now this might look a bit complex at first, but it's actually extremely simple. Ignore the exact syntax for now and just glance over what is actually happening. We are simply assigning information to keywords. We are just entering data that we want to assign to a term. We are saying that we want the animal's name to be Buster, and his type should be husky, etc. Then we are giving him a function to speak, which we are calling 'speak'. Simple enough, right? Let's break this down further one bit at a time and analyse the structure and syntax of an object.

So, first things first, you will notice we still use the var keyword followed by the name we want to call the variable, just like before. This variable is called 'animal', then we assign it to a piece of data, just like we have done previously. We use the = sign for this. After this things get a bit different. So to tell JavaScript that we want to create an object, we use curly braces, like so {}, then everything inside those curly braces is our object. You might also have noticed how defining an object spans over multiple lines, which is something we haven't really seen before, but this is absolutely fine when creating an object and helps to create wonderful, readable code that's easy to interpret and understand.

Now, an object is nothing more than a bunch of 'name: value' pairs. That is to say, we assign a value to a name of our choosing. Analysing the above example, let's take a closer look at the following snippet of code:

```
age: 6,
type: "Husky",
```

As you can see, we have created a name: value pair of age: 6 and type: 'Husky'. Notice how the words name and age are not in quotations? This is how you define a name for the pair: you specify it outside of any quotations. This imposes a restriction in that you must not have any spaces in your name, so camelCase is advised for terms. After you specify the name you must enter a colon to assign it to a value. In this case we are assigning it a number of 6 to age, and the word 'Husky' to the name of type. For the number, just as when we define a number variable, we omit the quotations, and likewise for the string 'Husky', we must use quotations just like we did when declaring our string variable. In the above example, after we have finished with our name: pair, we must enter a comma, which specifies that we have more name: value pairs to create. You must add a comma to the end of every name: value pair you create except the very last one in your object.

Skipping to the last name: value pair of our object, we can see the following code:

```
speak: function() {
console.log("Woof");
}
```

Here we are creating a function, which logs 'Woof!' to the console, and assigning this function to the name 'speak'. There is no need to name the function inside the function itself like we have historically, as the function will be accessible via the speak keyword.

And that's all there is to it. That's how you create an object. Now do you remember in the previous section when we broke down the difference between a property and a method, when we were looking at strings and numbers? Well now we can see in action exactly how you create those properties and methods. Looking again at our example you can see that each name: value pair is simply a property or a method on the variable (which is an object). Let's take a closer look to ensure we understand this.

```
var animal = {
name: "Buster", // property
age: 6, // property
type: "Husky", // property
colour: "blue", // property
// method
speak: function() {
console.log("Woof");
}
}
```

Notice how everything is a property, except the function, which is a method (while still also being a property). This is because the function performs an action, just like when we used the search() method before, it performed an action.

Think back to how we used the properties and methods of our strings and numbers earlier on in this chapter. How do you think you might get access to the age of the animal we have created here?

That's right, by making use of animal.age. By calling animal.age, we are saying to JavaScript 'look into the animal variable/object and give me the age'. Now let's think about if we wanted to call the speak method of the object? That's right, just as before, we simply call animal.speak() and JavaScript will perform the function in question and would log 'Woof!' to the console. Remember, parentheses must be added to run a function; in this instance if we leave off the parentheses, JavaScript would just return the function definition, meaning it would just show us the code used to create the function.

Another method for accessing an object's property is by using the following syntax: animal['name']; this is entirely identical to animal.name. It's entirely your choice as to which method you use.

And that's objects! Simple, powerful and effective. They can seem confusing at first, but in reality they are actually very simple. They are just buckets of data. If you are really struggling to conceptualize it, then simply just imagine them as a container for multiple variables. A way to store variables within variables.

Let's put what we have learned into practice with the following exercise:

Exercise

Open up your inspector tools in Google Chrome and head over to the console tab. Now create a new object named 'person'. Taking what we have seen with our animal object, create an object about yourself. Add in your own details as name: value pairs. Once you have finished adding your properties add one single method named 'speak' which simply outputs to the console 'Hello!' Now run person.speak() and confirm you have set up your object correctly.

What we have learned in this chapter

Well done – you have just learned one of the most important and challenging aspects of JavaScript. Put simply, if you understand objects, you understand a huge part of JavaScript. Congratulations – you can now claim to have an understanding of a programming language.

You've done fantastically well to have kept up so far. I know these concepts can seem a little daunting at first, but once you break them down into bitesize chunks, they are actually very tame. Take your time and go at your own pace. Never feel that you can't look back through the previous chapters to help you achieve and complete the exercises – it's so important that you understand each of these concepts as much as you can before moving on, as each concept builds on top of the foundations laid by the previous concepts. Objects are so important in JavaScript, so take the time to make sure that you understand them until the point where looking at the syntax feels like second nature. I encourage you to go off and create some other objects. Why not create one for a car or for a musical instrument? Start thinking in a more programmatically minded way about how to transpose real-life objects into a JavaScript object. Getting into the mindset of a programmer is so important on the journey to understanding JavaScript and becoming a fantastic web developer. You're doing great – keep it up!

09
JavaScript Part 3
Scope, arrays and loops

Scope

Let's now turn our focus to scope. Scope is probably a term you haven't come across before so let's start by defining exactly what scope is. Scope is effectively an understanding of access control. It helps us to understand how accessible certain variables are. This basically means how and where we are able to use our variables that we create. Let's kick off with a basic example of something called 'local scope':

```
function exampleFunction() {
var name = "John"
// Can use the variable 'name' here
}
// Can not use the variable 'name' here
```

Looking at the above example you can see that inside of the function, it is perfectly possible to make use of the variable 'name'; however, outside of the brackets of that function, we are unable to make use of the same variable. This is because of scope. Basically, because the variable was created *inside* the function, the variable can only be used inside of that function. It is said to become local to the function. It is a local variable with local scope and, as such, can only be accessed from within the function. Let's compare this to the following example:

```
var name = "John"
function exampleFunction() {
// Can use the variable 'name' here
}
// Can use the variable 'name' here
```

Notice how the variable can now be used anywhere, regardless of inside or outside of the function. This is because the variable was declared *outside* of any functions. It is a global variable, and therefore is said to have global scope. All scripts and functions can now access and make use of this variable.

Arrays

When programming, there are times when you will want to assign multiple values of the same type at once. If we used variables for this, it might look like this:

```
var name = "John";
var name2 = "Peter";
var name3 = "Carl"
```

This can be problematic and has limited uses. What if we wanted to count all of the names that we just assigned? If all the variables are names, wouldn't it be useful to combine them all into one single variable? Enter arrays. Simply put, an array is a variable that contains multiple values. Let's jump straight into an example to better highlight how arrays work:

```
var names = ["John", "Peter", "Carl"];
```

As you can see, we declare an array using square brackets [] with a list of values inside it. Just like with objects, the commas are important. They denote that there is another item after the current one. Just like with objects, we can make use of spaces and line breaks to help format our code. Take the above example. We can very easily write this as:

```
var names = [
"John",
"Peter",
"Carl"
];
```

and the end result would be identical. Any spaces outside of quotations are ignored with arrays, just like with objects.

You might be wondering how we work with an array. With objects we use the object.property notation in order to gain access to a value, so how do we do that with arrays when they don't have any key names? Well, the answer is simple: we use what we call an 'index number'. Every time we add a value to an array, it gets assigned a number, which auto increments from 0. Therefore, the very first item in any array, will have the index number of 0. Let's see an example of this:

```
var names = [
"Paul",    // Index number 0
"Peter",   // Index number 1
"Carl"     // Index number 2
];
```

As you can see from the above example, the first item in the array has the index of 0 and then every subsequent item gets assigned an index number one greater than the one before. What relevance is the index number? Well, the index number is how we pick off a single value from an array. How we do this is actually very simple, as we can see from the following syntax:

```
var
names = [
"Paul",  // Index number 0
"Peter", // Index number 1
"Carl"   // Index number 2
];

var secondName = names[1]; // variable will be set to
"Peter"
```

Analysing the example, we can see that we have created an array with the values 'John', 'Peter' and 'Carl'. Then we assign the variable secondName to the second value in the array 'names'.

At any point after the creation of an array, we can manually set the value of a position in the array by simply passing the data to the array's position, like so:

```
var names = [
"Paul", // Index number 0
"Peter", // Index number 1
"Carl" // Index number 2
];

names[1] = "Ted"
```

In the above example, the array would now have the following values 'Paul', 'Ted', 'Carl'. By passing a new value to the position in the array, we overwrite the existing value for that position.

Just like objects, arrays are very powerful, and just as is the case with objects we are not limited to just passing in strings. We can pass in any data type we like; we can pass in a string, a number, a date or even another object.

Let's explore an example together of how this is possible:

```
var animal = {
name: "Rolley",
colour: "brown",
age: 12
}
var arrayOfThings = [
"Paul", animal, 22
];
```

In the above example, we have assigned a string, an object and a number to our array, but we could take this even further. We could add a function to the array, or we could even assign another array to the array. There is no limit to the possibilities that this versatility affords us.

Exercise

Before I wrap up this section on arrays, let's take a quick break to test out our knowledge and push our brains a little bit. Let's see if you can put together the principles from what we have learned of JavaScript so far, in order to complete this exercise.

- Open up Chrome inspector tools and head over to the console.
- Create an object containing information about an animal.
- Create a new array and pass this object into the array at a position of your choosing.
- Now attempt to log to the console one of the values from your object, but by accessing it through your array.

The final step of this exercise asks you to perform something that we haven't discussed yet. However, using the principles that we have learned about JavaScript so far, some assumptions can be made as to how we might achieve the end result. Did you manage to work it out? If so, great work – you're clearly starting to understand how JavaScript operates and how we access and manipulate variables. If you didn't get it, it's no problem at all. This was something entirely new to you, so it's not a concern as long as you understand the solution you are about to see and how and why it works.

```
var animal = {
name: "Rolley",
colour: "brown",
age: 12
}
var arrayOfThings = [
"Paul", animal, 22
];

console.log(arrayOfThings[1].name); // Logs "Rolley"
```

If you're wondering what's going on in the last statement of this solution, then allow me to break it down for you. The first part of the parameter that we pass to the console.log function, is arrayOfThings[1]. This locates and retrieves the second position in our array, which is assigned to our object. Now that we have our object, we can use the '.name' syntax to pick a value off of our object. In this case we request the value of the 'name' variable. Which then returns the value 'Rolley', which then gets printed to the screen.

In JavaScript we can continue this process of using the .name notation to chain on further actions. Let's see another example where we might want to perform an action on that value. Let's say we want to find out the length of the name. We can simply add on

.length to the end of our statement, which will then look into the value and return its character count, just like so:

```
console.log(arrayOfThings[1].name.length); // Logs 6
```

What's good here is that the returned value, which in this case is 6, is of the data type number, even though we started out with an array. This means we can then take things one step further and perform arithmetic on the number, like this:

```
console.log(arrayOfThings[1].name.length+4); // Logs 10
```

Amazing, right? We can continue to add on methods or properties at will to manipulate and change the request until we get back what we are looking for.

This is a core principle of JavaScript so it's vitally important to understand this before moving on. Please do try this out for yourself in the console on Google Chrome. Play around with manipulating your response by adding on various properties, methods and so on to help yourself become more familiar with how it works.

Array methods and properties

Arrays, being objects (like almost everything is in JavaScript), allow us to make use of some built-in methods and properties. These methods can really help with how we make use of arrays. Let's dive straight in.

Length property

This one we've seen before: it counts the number of characters in a string. So what do you think it will do on an array? You might assume that it will count the number of characters of all the strings inside the array. But that's not quite right (largely because that wouldn't be particularly useful), it simply counts how many items exist inside the array. Simple enough, but let's see it in action:

```
var typicalArray = [
"Frank",
"Paul",
"Peter"
];
var arraySize = typicalArray.length // value is 3
```

Nice and simple, without any strange quirks. Imagine if all of JavaScript was that straightforward!

Adding elements to an array

You might be wondering what you might do if you create an array and want to add another value to the array later on. Arrays wouldn't be much use if you weren't able to add elements to them once they had been created, which is why JavaScript has a method for this exact purpose. It's called the push() method. It's a nice and descriptive method, which is very easy to use. You just need to call the method on the array, and pass in your element as a parameter. Let's see an example of the method in action:

```
var typicalArray = [
"Frank",
"Paul",
"Peter"
];
typicalArray.push("Carl"); // Adds 'Carl' to the end of
the array
```

The push method will always add the new element to the very end of the array. The push method is actually identical to doing the following:

```
typicalArray[typicalArray.length]= "Carl"; // Adds
'Carl' to the end of the array
```

Both methods of adding an element to the end of an array will produce the exact same result, only the push method is slightly more distinct and the preferred method because of its ease, simplicity and declarative nature (remember, when we write our code, a main aim of ours is always to write easy to interpret code).

Arrays really become powerful when we make the most of their methods. Here are some examples of the methods that are available to us every time we create a new array.

toString()

The toString method extracts the values of an array into to a comma separated list. It's important to note that when using this method, the resulting string will not have any spaces added between elements.

Example:

```
var myArray = [
"Frank",
"Paul",
"Peter"
];

// This logs to the console "Frank,Paul,Peter"
console.log(myArray.toString());
```

sort()

The sort method will sort the elements of an array alphabetically. You can also reverse the order of the sort, so that the result is reverse-alphabetical by using the reverse() method.

Example:

```
var myArray = [
"Frank",
"Paul",
"Peter",
"Adam"
];

// This logs to the console "Adam,Frank,Paul,Peter"
console.log(myArray.sort());

// This logs to the console "Peter,Paul,Frank,Adam"
console.log(myArray.reverse());
```

join()

The join method is similar to the toString method, in that it outputs your array as a string. However, with the join method, you are able to specify which character you want to use as the delimiter, where the toString method forces a comma. By using the join method instead of the toString method, we are able to force a space in between our elements, as can be seen in the example below:

```
var myArray = [
"Frank",
"Paul",
"Peter",
"Adam"
];

// This logs to the console "Frank, Paul, Peter, Adam"
console.log(myArray.join(", "));
```

pop()

The pop method can be seen as the opposite to the push method; instead of adding an element to the end of an array, the pop method allows us to remove the last element from an array. As well as removing the element, the method also 'returns' the element that was removed, meaning that we are able to use the method to remove the last element, and then see exactly what that element was. Take a look at how powerful this can be below:

```javascript
var myArray = [
"Frank",
"Paul",
"Peter",
"Adam"
];

var x = myArray.pop();
// This logs to the console "Adam was removed from the
array"
console.log(x + " was removed from the array");
```

shift()

The shift method is identical to the pop method, only instead of removing the element from the end of the array, it removes it from the front. Other than this small difference, its use and execution is identical to the pop method.

```javascript
var myArray = [
"Frank",
"Paul",
"Peter",
"Adam"
```

```
];
var x = myArray.shift();
// This logs to the console "Frank was removed from the
array"
console.log(x + " was removed from the array");
```

unshift()

The unshift method is identical to the push method, only instead of adding your new element to the end of the array, it adds it to the start of the array.

```
var myArray = [
"Frank",
"Paul",
"Peter",
"Adam"
];
// Adds Carl to start of array
myArray.unShift("Carl");
```

These methods allow us complete control over our array at any point onwards from its creation. These methods can be joined together to perform complex actions and manipulations on our arrays. There is no end to the possible combinations you could use to maintain your arrays. For example, you might want to sort the array alphabetically, and finally return the last item in the array before removing it. This complex action could be written in one single statement by chaining these powerful methods together. Let's see this in action before we move on.

```
var myArray = [
"Frank",
"Paul",
"Peter",
"Adam"
];

/* Sorts the array alphabetically, then removes the last
item, which gets set as the value of the x variable */
var x = myArray.sort().pop();
console.log(x); // Logs "Peter" to the console
```

Arrays vs objects

A large source of confusion for new programmers is around the differences between arrays and objects and when to use either of them. The answer is very simple. The two are largely identical, with one major difference. That difference is that arrays use numbers as their indexes, while objects use names as their indexes. What this really means is that when you are working with very structured data, an object is going to be better, while working with something a little simpler and linear, an array is going to be better.

A shopping list, for example, would lend itself well to an array, while details about a car would be much better suited to an object where we can detail the specific values and assign them to a name.

```
// Array with linear, list-like data
var shoppingList = ["Milk", "Sugar", "Cheese", "Butter"];

// Object with highly structured data
var car = {
make: "Ford",
colour: "Red",
mileage: 13000
}
```

Exercise

Let's conclude this section by solidifying our knowledge of arrays with a quick exercise making use of what we have learned so far about the power of arrays:

- Start by opening up Google Chrome and heading over to the console tab in inspector tools.
- Now create an array of your favourite films.
- Change the second to last item in your array to a different value.
- Now remove the first item in your array but save the value to a variable
- Sort the array reverse-alphabetically.
- Find out the size of your array and assign that value to a variable.
- Now log the following statement to the console, replacing the square brackets with actual data from the array: 'This is my array of my favourite things [List array of things separated by ' - ']. There are [size of array] items in my array, and i just removed [Removed value] from the list'.

Loops

We have just explored arrays and their uses. We looked at examples of shopping lists and lists of favourite things. We also looked at retrieving that information back out of arrays and assigning it to a variable. This is useful for individual elements, but what about when we are working with large arrays with lots of data? Imagine for a second that we have a huge list of people's dates of birth, and from that list we wanted to create a new list of people's ages. If we had five elements in that array, we could easily retrieve each of these elements, work out their age from their date of birth, then add that age to a new array. For five elements this might not take too long. Now what would you do if we have 500 elements in an array? You might want to find a way to speed that process up. What if we could write some code that would automatically sort through an entire array and perform a specified action on each individual item inside it? All by running one single command? Or what if you have an array of objects that contains all of your navigation bar's titles and destination links, which you need to iterate through and output to the webpage? Ladies and gentlemen, I give you 'loops', and with loops I also present to you the power of programming as a huge time-saver and the height of convenience. You are about to see why programming really is so powerful.

The loops

As we just discovered, loops are a way of performing an action multiple times in a programmatic way. They are a way to run a piece of code multiple times as per your requirements. They are often used alongside arrays, but their uses span far beyond just working with arrays. There are four different types of loops in JavaScript. The most common loop you will see is the 'for loop'. Let's take a closer look at this loop now.

The for loop

The for loop is a very common loop, which simply runs a section of code a defined number of times. Here's how it works:

```
for(statement 1; statements 2; statement 3) {
}
```

This is the basic structure of the for loop. We start with the keyword 'for', followed by three statements, which define how many times our loop runs.

Statement 1 is a piece of code you will write that will be run BEFORE the loop runs.

Statement 2 is a condition statement, which will decide whether or not the loop should run.

Statement 3 is a piece of code you will write that will be run AFTER your code inside the loop is run.

Let's look at an example and break down exactly how it all works:

```
for(var i = 0; i < 10; i++) {
console.log(i);
}
```

The above loop will run for 10 times exactly and then stop. Here's what's going on here:

- Var i = 0

  This code declares a variable called i, and sets it equal to 0. This code runs before any loops are run. This section is only ever run once at the start of the loop process.

- i < 10

  The loop then checks this statement to see if it returns true. This statement in question is 'Is the variable i less than the value 10?' Because our variable i is set to 0, this will return TRUE, and so the loop will run. The statement here is what's known as a condition. We will explore more about conditions later.

- i++

  After the block of code inside the curly brackets is run, this is then executed. Remember when we see this i++ it is an arithmetic operation, that is the equivalent to i = i + 1. The code here simply adds 1 to our i variable. You can perform any operation here; you are not just limited to adding 1.

- {
  console.log(i)
  }

This is the code that will be executed each time our loop is run. The loop order of events is as follows:

- i variable is set to 0.

- Loop checks if statement is TRUE (i is less than 10 so result is TRUE).

- Block of code is executed – console.log(i) is run. i is equal to 0 so "0" will be outputted.

- i++ is run, setting i to the value of 1.

- Loop checks if statement is TRUE (i is set to 1, so still less than 10, thus TRUE).

- Block of code is executed – console.log(i) i is equal to 1 so "1" will be outputted.

- i++ is run, setting i to the value of 2.

- Repeat until i is set to 10, at which point the condition statement becomes FALSE and the next line of the JavaScript script is then run.

It's important to understand that when we define our condition statement, we must define a condition that can 'break' or the loop will run forever. This just means that we must write a condition that will at some stage return FALSE as a result of our loop running.

Let's see a for loop in the context of looping through an array and picking off values.

```
var myArray = ["John", "Callum", "Paul", "Frank"];
for(var i = 0; i < myArray.length; i++) {
console.log(myArray[i]);
}
```

Can you work out for yourself what is going on here? Have a go at working your way through the loop, deciphering what is happening here and what the expected output will be.

Now let's break it down together. Let's see the code again, this time with some comments:

```javascript
// Declare an array
var myArray = ["John", "Callum", "Paul", "Frank"];
// If i is less than the value of the size of the array
(4), then run the code
for(var i = 0; i < myArray.length; i++) {
// Log to the console the array with the index position
that's the same as the value of i
console.log("Hello my name is " + myArray[i]);
}
```

Hopefully the comments give an insight into what is happening here, but let's talk through it anyway. We first declare an array, just like we have done many times in the past. Then the loop we have written will run for a total of four times, which we defined with our condition statement i < myArray.length.

This statement is the same as writing i < 4, however, because we have set the condition equal to the size of the array. If you ever want to add data to the array, you won't need to rewrite this loop, as the loop's condition statement has been dynamically set.

Each time the loop runs we output the statement 'Hello my name is [name]', [name] being replaced by the value of the element in that position in the array. Therefore, after this loop has run, the console would look like this:

Hello my name is John
Hello my name is Callum
Hello my name is Paul
Hello my name is Frank

Yet we only wrote the code once. How powerful is that? We were able to dynamically create a bunch of statements from a small snippet of code. This is the principle of programming. We are writing small chunks of code to carry out complex operations for us that we would otherwise have to do manually. Seriously, how great is programming?

When writing for loops it is important to consider that all three statements are optional; you can omit any one of them and the loop will still run. Just make sure that you write a condition for the loop to break or the loop will run endlessly and crash the system, so realistically you wouldn't ever want to leave out the second condition statement.

The for/in loop

This loop is used for looping through the properties of an object. Similar to the standard for loop, it is used to iterate through and perform an action on each individual property of an object. Its syntax is nice and succinct. It's an easy loop to use and understand, so let's breeze through it nice and quickly.

```
var car = {
make: "Ford",
model: "Fiesta",
colour: "Blue"
};
var x;
for(x in car) {
console.log(car[x]);
}
```

As you can see, after we have defined our object, we first declare a new variable named x – this is going to be used during our loop. Then we use a standard for keyword, followed by the parenthesis which contains the code 'x in car'. In this loop, the value of x is set to that of each property, so when we step into the actual code to be executed, inside the curly braces, we can see that we are making use of the x variable to pick off that property from the car object and display it in the console.

Similarly to the standard for loop, we can write any code that we wish inside this block. The loop will automatically iterate through the whole object until it reaches the end of the properties.

This loop is an automatic loop, which requires very little code in order to achieve a very powerful loop.

The while loop

The while loop is similar in nature to the for loop, in that they both run a block of code if a condition is true. However, the way they go about this is slightly different between the two.

With the while loop, we specify our condition at the top, just like in the for loop. However, that's all we need to do. We simply define the criteria that we want to be true for the code to run, then we handle the variable changing inside the block. This allows us a bit more flexibility than when using the for loop, as we can decide exactly where we would like to place our variable incrementing statement, just as we can see below:

```
while(x < 10) {
console.log(x);
x++;
}
```

The general rule for deciding between using a for loop and a while loop is as follows.

If you know the exact number of iterations you want your loop to run for, then use a for loop; if you have a rough idea about how many times you want the loop to run, but don't know the exact number, then a while loop is better suited.

The do/while loop

The do/while loop is a variation on the while loop, in which we are able to write a loop that is guaranteed to always run at least once. Looking at the syntax we can see why this is the case:

```
do {
console.log(x);
x++;
}
while(x < 10);
```

As you can see, in a do/while loop, the do statement comes first, therefore is always run at least once. This loop works exactly as the name suggests: the code will do (execute) the block of code inside curly braces, while the condition is TRUE.

As you can probably tell by now, all of these loops are very similar, with minor differences between them. Each has their own specific use-case, but generally you are most likely to be making use of the for loop. Now, let's write some loops.

Exercise

Loops are everywhere in programming, it's important to practise writing them until they become second nature to you, so let's spend some time writing a few loops and trying out the different ways of achieving our desired results.

- Open up Google Chrome and head over to your console in inspector tools.
- Create an array of your choosing with at least five values.
- Write a loop to loop through the array and log to the console its values.
- Write another loop to loop through the array in REVERSE order.
- Write one final loop, which loops through your array, but is guaranteed to run at least once, regardless of the array's length.

Make sure you get the desired outcome for each loop before moving on. Loops are a fundamental part of programming and it's vitally important that you are fully comfortable with how they work.

What we have learned in this chapter

Before we move on to the next chapter, let's recap exactly what we have just learned. We have taken a deep look into the power of arrays and understood exactly how they work along with their uses and functionality. We explored the built-in methods and values that come along with any array we create, before creating many of our own arrays and manipulating them at will. We have seen how to add, remove, change and sort our arrays to our requirements. We took a deep look at all of the methods we might want to use with our arrays before finally considering the differences between arrays and objects and their very similar nature, yet very different uses.

We have also covered loops. Loops are actually pretty simple, despite how powerful they are. While they can seem quite complex, there are just four of them, which all do pretty much the same thing, albeit in their own unique, slightly different way. They help to cover all use-cases of ways to loop through your data, and it is always better to have more ways to do something than none at all. Spend some time getting especially familiar with the standard for loop before moving on. The for loop will be the one you see the most out there in the wild. So there we have it, you understand loops! You're one step closer to becoming a fully fledged web developer. Loops are a core piece of the JavaScript (and general programming) puzzle and they are used everywhere, so feel proud of yourself for getting to grips with them. They are powerful little things that will allow you to create all manner of interesting algorithms for manipulating your arrays and objects. Never underestimate the power of the loops. In the next chapter, we are going to explain a bit more about how the condition statements inside these loops work.

This chapter was probably the most difficult we have seen so far and certainly put our understanding of JavaScript to the test. To have made it this far already is an achievement, but don't stop just yet. We are about to explore a huge part of programming that takes your arrays and makes use of them in a plethora of ways. We are about to see how much time programming can save us when working with data as we move on to the fourth and final part of the JavaScript section.

10
JavaScript Part 4

What we will learn in this chapter

This is the final part of the JavaScript section. We are going to cover Boolean values, comparisons, conditional statements and events.

Boolean values

In the previous section, when we took a look at loops, we saw some comparison statements for the first time. In these comparison statements, we saw how if the statement returned TRUE, the loop would run and when it returned FALSE, it would not run. Well, these TRUE and FALSE values have a name and their own data type – they are referred to as Boolean values. Booleans are a data type that can only ever be TRUE or FALSE. In JavaScript everything is either TRUE or FALSE. Let's look at exactly what that means now.

In JavaScript, everything has a value of either true or false, whether it be a string, an object, a variable, an expression. Let's take a look at some examples of things that return true in JavaScript.

- Numbers (1, 50, 200).
- Strings ("Hi There").
- Valid Expressions (1 < 10).

As you can see, these all have a value, and thus are true. Conversely, anything without a value will return false. Some examples of things that return false are:

- The Number 0 (0 and –0).
- Empty strings ("").
- Undefined variables (var x;).
- The value null (var x = null).
- False values (var x = false).
- NaN not a number variable (var x = "Hi" / 20).

Because everything in JavaScript is either true or false, it allows us to use anything as a condition for a condition statement. This brings us nicely on to the topic of comparisons.

Comparisons

Comparisons in JavaScript are exactly as their name implies – they are ways of analysing and comparing different things in JavaScript to determine equality or difference in the statement. If something is 'correct' it is true; if incorrect, it's false.

Let's compare some statements against a variable we will now define with a value of 10:

```
var x = 10
```

Now let's use this variable for comparison to see how different statements are analysed (see Table 10.1).

Table 10.1   How different statements are analysed

Operator	Meaning	Description	Examples

==	Equal to	Determines if two values are the same	x == 10 // TRUE
			x == 1 // FALSE
			x == –1 // FALSE
			x == "1" // TRUE

(continued)

Table 10.1 (Continued)

Operator	Meaning	Description	Examples

===	Equal value as well as type	This one checks to ensure that two values are both the same value as well as the same data type	x == 10 // TRUE
			x == "10" // FALSE

!=	Is not equal to	Checks to see if values are NOT the same. If they are not the same, it returns TRUE	x != 1 // TRUE x != 10 // FALSE
!==	Is not equal to or not the same type	Checks to see if values are NOT the same. If they are not the same, or are not the same type TRUE	x !== 1 // TRUE x !== "10" // TRUE x !== 10 // FALSE
>	Greater than	Checks to see if the value on the left side of the > is greater than the value on the right side. Returns TRUE if so	x > 1 // TRUE x > 20 // FALSE
<	Less than	Checks to see if the value on the left side of the < is less than the value on the right side. Returns TRUE if so	x < 20 // TRUE x < 10 // FALSE
>=	Greater than or equal to	Checks to see if the value on the left side of the >= is greater than or the same as the value on the right side. Returns TRUE if so	x >= 10 // TRUE x >= 11 // FALSE
<=	Less than or equal to	Checks to see if the value on the left side of the <= is less than or the same as the value on the right side. Returns TRUE if so	x <= 10 // TRUE x <= 9 // FALSE

Comparison operators are great for allowing us the ability to compare values in order to satisfy a condition. This opens up a world of possibilities for a programmer, who can create many 'if this is the case, then do this' operations in their code and, as such, create complex and powerful applications, which can respond to changes accordingly. At a basic level, this is what happens every time you log into any website. A check happens against your username and password; if they match the expected result, the statement returns TRUE and you are able to log in.

If the power of these comparison operators wasn't already enough, we can also join them together to form complex queries that ask multiple questions. We can use the following logical operators to join conditional statements together to form complex queries like so:

```
1 < 10 && 5 < 10
```

As you can see from the above example, we have joined together two comparisons, 1< 10 and 5 < 10 by making use of the && logical operator.

The && logical operator simply says 'and' so we can read the above statement as follows: 'if 1 is less than 10 and 5 is less than 10 then return TRUE.' Both of the conditions must be met in order for it to return true, so the following statement would return FALSE.

```
1 < 10 && 5 > 10
```

Joining these comparison operators together is great and allows us more control over when and how our code is run; however, they do not satisfy every demand – what about situations where we might want to say 'if this or this is true, then return true'? Enter the || operator.

```
1 < 10 || 5 > 10
```

This example will return TRUE as one of the conditions is met (1 is less than 10). Remember the above statement can be read as such: 'if 1 is less than 10 or 5 is greater than 10 then return TRUE.' This allows us to write more flexible queries that apply to more use-cases, making them more reusable, and thus helping us to write fewer lines of code.

All this is great and everything, but you're probably wondering how we actually use these comparison operators. Well, we can make use of them in conditional statements. What's a conditional statement? It's only one of the most important aspects of all programming languages...

Conditional statements

Conditional statements allow us to write code that gets executed when certain conditions are met. They enable us to write code that reacts and responds to changes and is dynamic in nature. We are able to do this through the use of four different conditional statements. This is another area of JavaScript where it's much easier to see it in action, rather than explain. So let's jump straight in with an example of an if statement.

The if statement

If statements are quite literally a block of code that will run if a statement is true. The syntax is nice and succinct, and very descriptive.

```
if(1 < 5) {
console.log('Condition is true');
}
```

Looking at the above code it is fairly self-explanatory. The statement outlines that if 1 is less than 5, then the code inside the block should run, and log 'Condition is true' to the console.

This is as complex as standard if statements get. They simply run if the statement inside the parenthesis returns true. If statements will only run the block of code once, unlike a loop, which will run it a number of times.

To write an if statement, you simply write the keyword 'if' (this keyword is case sensitive, so always lowercase 'if' as using uppercase will throw an error) followed by parenthesis. Inside the parentheses you can write just about anything you like and pass in any variables from outside of the statement if you wish. The only clause is that if you don't write a condition that can't be validated to true, the block of code will never run. After the parenthesis, and our condition, we write our code to be executed inside the curly braces. This code can be anything again, and can use the variables that were pulled in, global, or created inside the parenthesis. Then, during execution of the code, when the code reaches the if statement, JavaScript will determine whether the condition is met (if it returns TRUE), and if it is it will execute the code inside the block one time.

There is no end to the statements and code combinations you could write. The if statement is one of the most powerful aspects of JavaScript – it allows us to be the masters of our own code and create an application that is intelligent, dynamic and knows how to respond to various conditions.

Else statement

The else statement is an adjunctive to the if statement. You can't have an else without an if. The else statement simply says, 'if the main condition isn't met, then do this.' The statement will question 'if this is true, do this, else do this'. Quite expressive. The formatting of an else statement is very simple – it follows immediately from the closing curly brace of an if statement and contains the simple keyword 'else' followed by its own set of curly braces which will contain the code to be run if the main condition isn't satisfied. Let's look at an example below following on from our if statement.

```
if(1 < 5) {
console.log('Condition is true');
} else {
console.log('Condition is false');
}
```

Adding an else statement to your if statement ensures that a piece of code always runs, regardless of whether the statement is true or not. This can be useful when responding to a query. Let's imagine that we have a website that contains a list of books and a user is searching for a certain book. We can write an if else statement that checks whether there is a match for the book, and if there isn't one, responds with a message to inform the user of this.

The else if statement

This statement fits between the if clause and else clause of a conditional statement. This part is responsible for running an alternative condition if the first one isn't met. You can chain multiple else if statements together to form a flow in your code. Let's see an example, then we can explain it in more detail:

```
var number = 15
if(number < 5) {
console.log('Your number is between 0 and 4');
} else if(number < 10) {
console.log('Your number is between 5 than 9');
} else if(number < 15) {
console.log('Your number is between 10 than 14');
} else {
console.log('Your number is over 15');
}
```

As you can see in the above code, we have chained multiple if else statements together to form a flow. Imagine this piece of code like a waterfall, which runs from the top down. It first checks the first if statement; if the condition is met, it will run the code inside the curly braces, and then the execution of the if statement as a whole will stop and move on to the next section of your code; however, if the first statement is not true, it will not execute that first block of code, instead it will fall down to the next else if statement, and check that condition to see if it's true. If it is, then that code gets executed. If not, once again it falls down to the next if else. It continues this flow all the way through the if statement until it either finds a condition that is true, reaches an else statement or reaches the end of the statement entirely (in which case nothing will happen and JavaScript will just move on to the next statement).

Looking at the above code, can you have a guess which piece of code will be executed, and what will be logged to the console? Feel free to create this exact scenario in your browser to test this out yourself. Did you guess right? The correct answer is 'Your number is 15 or over'. This is because, as we work our way through the if statement, none of the if or else if statements render true. The closest one to being true is the final else if (number < 15), but our number is 15, so it's not less than 15, it's equal to 15, therefore none of the if statements run, instead the else statement runs, logging 'Your number is 15 or over' to the console.

If statements, when combined with else if and else statements, allow us complete control and flexibility over our code and how it runs. We can control every possibility, as long as we code for it.

The slight problem with the if statement and all of its corresponding else if statements, is that when we have a large number of different conditions that we need to consider, the code can get quite messy and unruly. This makes debugging hard as it's not always easy to decipher exactly what is going on. For situations with a small number of outcomes, an if statement is perfect. However, for more complex queries, we need something a little bit more adept at handling multiple cases. For this, we need the switch statement.

The switch statement

This conditional statement is perfect for situations where we have a large number of different actions that should be performed based on different conditions being met. The switch statement has different syntax to anything we have seen before. It can seem a little strange at first, so let's waste no time in getting familiar with it. Let's see some code:

```javascript
var number = 15;

switch(number) {
case 5:
console.log('number is 5');
break;
case 10:
console.log('number is 10');
break;
case 15:
console.log('number is 15');
}
```

Looking at the above code, there's a lot of new syntax to analyse here, so let's work our way from top to bottom.

- We start with the keyword switch followed by parenthesis.

- Inside the parenthesis we enter our expression. (The expression is the value that we want to evaluate our cases against. So in this case we just enter the variable number. This means that every case inside the switch statement will be evaluated against the number 15.)

- Then we move down to the case keyword followed by the test case, so in the first example we are using 'case 5'. This is saying: 'if the number is 5 then this case is true.'

- This is followed by a colon, not a semi-colon, which is something we have only seen before in objects.

- Then on a new line we enter our code that we want to run when the case is true.

- After we finish writing our code, we follow it up with a break keyword followed by a semi-colon. The break keyword instructs JavaScript to 'break' out of the switch block and stop the execution of any more code inside the switch statement.

- After our break keyword, we can write another case directly below, with the same syntax.

During execution of the code, JavaScript will handle the switch statement very much like an if else statement. It will look for a single valid condition that returns TRUE, execute that code, then move on to the next section of your code outside of the statement.

You will notice that the final case in the switch statement doesn't contain a break. This is because the code will stop here anyway, as this is not a loop, and as soon as JavaScript has worked its way through your statement, it will move on, even if it doesn't find a match.

In the current state of our switch statement, it is entirely possible for there to be no matches, and therefore no code is executed. If we want to emulate the else functionality of an if statement, and mitigate against a situation where no matches are found, we can make use of the default keyword. The default keyword is largely identical to the else section of an if statement, in that it is run if no other match is found.

To use the default keyword, we simply add it into our switch statement, like so:

```
var number = 15;

switch(number) {
case 5:
console.log('number is 5');
break;
case 10:
console.log('number is 10');
```

```
break;
case 15:
console.log('number is 15');
break;
default:
console.log('No match found');
}
```

An important detail to note is that you don't need to position the default statement at the end of the statement – you could even position it at the very top. As long as it's inside the switch statement, its position in the flow is irrelevant.

```
var number = 15;

switch(number) {
default:
console.log('No match found');
break;
case 5:
console.log('number is 5');
break;
case 10:
console.log('number is 10');
break;
case 15:
console.log('number is 15');
}
```

Sometimes when writing a switch statement, you will come across a situation where you might want multiple cases to perform the same action. Switch statements make this very easy. You can simply chain together multiple case statements before your code, then that code will be assigned to both cases. Let's see what we mean by this with an example.

```
var number = 15;

switch(number) {
default:
console.log('No match found');
break;
case 5:
case 10:
console.log('number is 5 or 10');
break;
case 15:
console.log('number is 15');
}
```

As you can see, we have 'chained' together case 5 and case 10, which means that if number is equal to either 5 or to 10, then the same code will run. This helps to keep our code nice and clean, which makes it easier to interpret and debug, which, as we've established, is incredibly important.

So that's conditional statements for you. It is a powerful, core part of JavaScript, and all programming languages for that matter. It can't be overstated how much of a huge part of JavaScript conditional statements make up. You will struggle to find any JavaScript code that doesn't contain at least one conditional statement. They are so useful and actually quite easy to write and work with. Now that you understand them, you are so close to being able to claim that you understand all of the core aspects of JavaScript. We have one small section left, before we can put everything we have learned into practice as we go off and create our first dynamic website. Lastly for JavaScript, let's look at events.

Events

It's important to remember that JavaScript's main purpose is to integrate with the browser and your website. JavaScript's tight integration with the browser is one of the main features of JavaScript.

The benefit of using JavaScript with your website is that we are able to write JavaScript code that can 'react' to certain 'events' that occur on your website.

What's an event? An event is simply something that a browser or a user does. Some examples of events are when a website has finished loading, when a button is clicked, when a user hovers over a div, when a form is submitted and so on. Using JavaScript, we can react to these events by executing code snippets that we define in advance.

We can 'tie' these actions to the events in our HTML. We can simply assign the action directly to the element we want to react to, like so:

```
<p id="text"></p>
<button onclick="document.getElementById('text').
innerHTML='Paul'">My name is?</button>
```

As you can see, to assign the action to the event of the button being clicked, we add an 'onclick' attribute to our HTML tag, followed by the JavaScript action in single or double quotations. The above example will enter the text "Paul" into the div with the id 'text' when the button is clicked.

As you can see in the above example, we are writing pure JavaScript directly into the attribute's value, which is fine for small snippets of JavaScript, but what about when we want to write more complex functions? It can quickly become troublesome. As such, it is common in JavaScript to assign functions to the attribute instead of code itself. Therefore, you are far more likely to see this:

```
<p id="text"></p>
<button onclick="showName()">My name is?</button>
<script>
function showName() {
document.getElementById('text').innerHTML='Paul'
}
</script>
```

This extracts the code out into its own function, which makes the code far more maintainable and easier to read. This is the preferred method of assigning actions to events.

As we established earlier, there are many different events that JavaScript can react to. The full list of events we can watch out for are as follows:

- Onchange. Event is triggered when an HTML element has been changed in some way, such as when a user has input some information into a web form.

- Onclick. Event is triggered when an HTML element is clicked. This can be any element, such as a div, a table, an image, etc.

- Onmouseover. Event is triggered when a user hovers their mouse over an HTML element; once again, this can be on any element.

- Onmouseout. Event is triggered when a user stops hovering over the HTML element. Again, this can run on any element and is usually paired with the onmouseover event.

- Onkeydown. Event is triggered when a user presses a key on their keyboard. This is a good event to watch for on forms.

- Onload. Event is triggered when the webpage has finished loading. This is good for when we want to wait for all of the images, etc, to finish generating their size on page load, so that we can perform operations based on their size attributes.

We can make use of any of these events by simply adding the event text to the responsible HTML element like we did before. Let's see a few examples of this in action.

```
<p id="text"></p>
<button onmouseover="showName()">My name is?</button>
<script>
function showName() {
document.getElementById('text').innerHTML='Paul'
}
</script>
```

In the above example, if the user hovers over the element, the action will be triggered, and the function will run, replacing the text with 'Paul' just like in the example before.

This integration between HTML and JavaScript allows us so much control over our webpage and enables us to create rich, dynamic experiences for our users.

We have only scratched the surface of event handling in JavaScript – there's a lot more going on with event handlers, which we will see again in the next chapter.

What we have learned in the JavaScript section

This chapter brings our journey through the basics of JavaScript to a close. We have covered a huge amount of information and worked our way through an incredible amount of sample code. Your journey towards becoming a web developer has taken a huge leap forward in this section.

You have explored the entire basics of a programming language that will transform your website from a simple, static page into a dynamic, living, breathing experience. You should feel incredibly proud of yourself for getting this far. It really is impressive and shows true determination that will serve you well in the future within the field of web design, where determination and resilience are fundamental traits of a successful programmer.

The next, and final, section will see us working through a series of instructions together to build our own website using everything we have learned so far. This will be our biggest test yet, but will also be the most rewarding. It will help you get familiar with writing the code you have seen in this book so far.

Part Four
Putting everything into practice

Everything we have learned so far has been leading to this section. We are about to put everything we know about building websites into practice. We are going to be taking every single one of the concepts we have covered, and we are going to make use of them here, while also introducing a few new concepts along the way, a few tips here and there and plenty of challenges to really test your skills. If there were any sections in this book that you didn't feel particularly comfortable with, now is a good time to go back and brush up on them, as the training wheels are off with this chapter and you will be left largely to your own devices to put into practice the challenges I set you.

Here's how it's going to work.

First, I will set a challenge and explain exactly what I want you to create, followed by the expected outcome of the challenge. After this, I will be supplying the actual method of how to achieve the desired outcome, followed by the expected code that you should have written. Try not to peek at this until you have given the challenge a good go yourself.

At the end of this section you will have a fully functional reference website, which will contain all of the core topics covered in this book, and provide you with an easy-to-use method of recalling any part of the book and what we have learned, going forward. Think of this website as a way for you to quickly recall an area of website building for your own knowledge when building websites in the future.

11
Creating the website

Setting things up

It's important that we are on the exact same setup for this chapter, as I will be introducing some tips along the way that you will really benefit from, going forward. So for clarity, I will be using Sublime Text as my text editor, Google Chrome as my browser and Photoshop as my image editor (you don't have to use Photoshop, but it would be ideal to mirror my setup as much as possible for the maximum benefit).

A quick note before we start: some of these challenges will be outside the scope of what we have learned so far and will stretch your knowledge and understanding of web design. In these circumstances, you can either have a go at working out the solution yourself, or you can google the challenge and find the answer that way. A huge part of web development is finding solutions to problems you face online. Learning how to google an issue you are having is a fundamental aspect of web design.

Great, now that we've got that out of the way, let's start coding!

The homepage

HTML

The template

Let's kick things off with the page template that we will be using for our homepage.

The steps:

- Create a new folder in a directory of your choosing, name it whatever you want.
- Head over to Sublime Text.
- Open the folder in Sublime Text (you should see an empty directory structure).
- Create a new file called index.html.
- Inside your index.html file create a template for our webpage, consisting of:
  - DOCTYPE declaration
  - html, head, and body tags
- Give your webpage a title of 'How to build a website'.
- Create a div with an id of 'introduction'.
- Inside the 'introduction' div:
  - add a header with the same text as your page title 'How to build a website'
  - add a paragraph and enter the following text snippet: 'This website contains a reference to everything I know about HTML, CSS and JavaScript. Each language is contained on its own page, and each section of the language is contained in a separate block. Use the main navigation and then the jump list to navigate straight to any section of the webpage.'

Expected result: the expected result of this should be a basic webpage with a simple header and paragraph explaining a bit about the website.

Expected code:

```
<!DOCTYPE html>
<html>
<head>
<title>How to build a website</title>
```

```
</head>
<body>

<div id="introduction">
<h1>How to build a website</h1>
<p>This website contains a reference to everything I
know about HTML, CSS and JavaScript. Each language is
contained on its own page, and each section of the
language is contained in a separate block. Use the main
navigation and then the jump list to navigate straight
to any section of the webpage.</p>
</div>

</body>
</html>
```

Navigation

We are now going to create the main navigation method for our website. We are going to create a horizontal nav bar that sits at the very top of every page.

The steps:

- Create a new div above the 'introduction' div and give it an id of 'navigation'.

- Inside the 'navigation' div add a new div and give it an id of 'navigation-inside'.

- Inside the 'navigation-inside' div add an unordered list with the following list items:

  - a relative link to 'index.html' with the text 'Home' and a class of 'active'

  - a relative link to 'html.html' with the text 'HTML'

  - a relative link to 'css.html' with the text 'CSS'

  - a relative link to 'javascript.html' with the text 'JavaScript'

Expected result: the expected result of this should be a list of hyperlinks that go to various pages (which do not yet exist). Currently the list will be rendering vertical and all the links should be blue (aside from the home link, which should be a darker shade to indicate the page is active).

Expected code:

```
<div id="navigation">
 <div id="navigation-inside">
  <ul>
    <li><a href="index.html" class="active">Home</a></li>
    <li><a href="html.html">HTML</a></li>
    <li><a href="css.html">CSS</a></li>
    <li><a href="javascript.html">JavaScript</a></li>
  </ul>
 </div>
</div>
```

Note: you should be checking your index.html file in your browser to see how it's taking shape. If you haven't done so already, please do check it out now. Not looking pretty, is it? Well, let's sort that out now with some images and then some styling to make it a bit easier on the eye.

Images

Let's now create a nice header image for our website to add a little more stimulation for our users. Header images are a great way to start off a webpage – they instantly add colour and softly ease your users into the actual content of the page without overwhelming them.

The steps:

- Inside your main folder create a new folder called 'img'.
- If you haven't already, download the source files from the link at the start of the book.

- Copy the 'header-image.jpg' and 'headshot.png' files and paste them into your 'img' folder.

- Back in Sublime Text add a div between the 'navigation' and the 'content' divs and give it an id of 'header'.

- Inside the 'header' div add the image 'header-image.jpg' to the site.

- Add a new div below the image and give it an id of 'profile'.

- Inside this div add another div with the id of 'profile-image'.

- Inside this div add the 'headshot.png' image.

- Below the image add an <h2> tag and enter the text 'by "your name"' inside the tags, replacing 'your name' with your actual name.

Expected result: after performing the above steps we should now have a nice header image and a profile icon on our website along with your name, all rendering to our webpage.

Expected code:

```
<div id="header">
<div id="profile">
<img src="img/header-image.jpg" alt="Header Image">
<div id="profile-image">
<img src="img/profile-icon.png" alt="Profile icon">
</div>
<h2>by Kenny Wood</h2>
</div>
</div>
```

Note: feel free to replace the profile icon with an actual picture of yourself. Just try to ensure that the image is cropped into a nice square that focuses on your head. A passport-type photo is what we're aiming for here.

Styling

Now that we have created our HTML for the page, we are going to need to style the page to make it appealing to the user. For this section you are free to experiment with your own colour choices – just try to stick to the same rules as me for the actual layout, other than that, go wild! Our goal here is to create a nice-looking webpage with a fixed header at the top of the page, which will remain at the top regardless of the user's position on the page, followed by a header image, which is then overlaid with your profile picture (or stock icon) and your name, followed by a content pane with a capped width that will help to ensure readability of our webpage (remember, long line-lengths make things difficult to read). Sounds confusing? Well then, let's break it down into a few step-by-step sections. Give it a good go yourself, and if you really can't manage, there's always the expected code at the end to look through.

Styling the template

Let's first style the navigation bar and page background.

The steps:

- Let's start by adding a new file called style.css in our root folder.
- Now add a link to this file in your index.html file.
- Open the style.css file in Sublime Text.
- Write rules to achieve the following desired output per element:
  - body

    remove all margins

    give it a background colour of '#eee'

    The font Arial, falling back to Helvetica, then sans-serif

  - #navigation

    make this a fixed element

    give it a nice and high z-index

position it at the top of the page

make the div the full width of the page

give it a white background

give the top and bottom a padding of 10px

- #navigation-inside

  give it a width of 600px

  make it float in the centre of the parent div

- #navigation-inside ul

  give it the full width of the parent div

  remove all list styles

  centre the text

  remove all margins and paddings

- #navigation-inside li

  give it a width of a quarter of its parent

  stack the list items side by side

- a

  give all links the colour '#333'

  remove the underline from all links

  make clicked or hovered links turn the colour '#1998E2'

- .active

  give it the colour '#1998E2'

Expected result: what we should now expect to see is a navigation bar fixed to the top of the page, with equally spaced out menu items with dark grey text, with the home tile coloured blue to indicate that it is the coloured page. The navigation background should be white, and the links should be contained to a maximum width of 600px. On hovering over one of the links, the link should turn blue to indicate that it is a link.

Expected code:

```css
body {
  margin: 0px;
  background: #eee;
  font-family: Arial, Helvetica, sans-serif;
}

#navigation {
  position: fixed;
  z-index: 9;
  top: 0;
  left: 0;
  width: 100%;
  background: white;
  padding: 10px 0px;
}

#navigation-inside {
  width: 600px;
  margin: 0 auto;
}

#navigation-inside ul {
  width: 100%;
  list-style: none;
  text-align: center;
  margin: 0px;
  padding: 0px;
}

#navigation-inside li {
  width: 25%;
  float: left;
}
```

```
a {
  color: #333;
  text-decoration: none;
}
a:active, a:hover {
  color: #1998E2;
}
.active {
  color: #1998E2;
  font-weight: bold;
}
```

Note: some of these concepts we haven't seen before, such as list-style overriding. Hopefully you were able to search online and find the solution to this issue by yourself. The only way to truly grow as a developer, is to accept that you can't ever know everything in this constantly evolving field, and that an essential part of becoming a good web developer is knowing how to find and learn ways of overcoming the issues you face with your code.

Styling the header

Let's now turn our focus to the header section of the page. The goal here is to create a full-width banner image, which is overlaid with a circular profile picture/icon, and your name. Part of this banner will sit underneath the navigation bar, as the navigation bar is fixed over the top of all of our content. This is fine and expected behaviour.

The steps:

Write rules to achieve the following desired output per element:

- #header
  - make the header the full width of the page
  - hide anything that overflows from the div
- #header img
  - give the image a width of 100% of its parent
  - set the height of the image to automatically adjust to preserve the aspect ratio

- #profile
  - give this div a width of 100px
  - set it to be absolutely positioned
  - give it a sensible z-index to show it on top of our content
  - centre the div horizontally
  - set the div to be 60px from the top of its parent element
- #profile-image
  - give this a height and width of 100px
  - using border radius, make this div a circle
  - make the background white
  - hide anything that flows outside of the element
- #profile-image img
  - give this image a width of 100%
  - set the height to automatically adjust
- #profile h2
  - make this text white
  - centre align the text
  - give it a font size of 14px

Expected result: after writing the necessary rules above to satisfy the challenges set, we should end up with a big and wide profile image with our profile icon centred over the top.

Expected code:

```
#header {
  width: 100%;
  overflow: hidden;
}

#header img {
  width: 100%;
```

```
  height: auto;
}

#profile {
  width: 100px;
  position: absolute;
  z-index: 1;
  left: 50%;
  margin-left: -50px;
  top: 60px;
}

#profile-image {
  width: 100px;
  height: 100px;
  border-radius: 50px;
  background: white;
  overflow: hidden;
}

#profile-image img {
  width: 100%;
  height: auto;
}

#profile h2 {
  color: white;
  text-align: center;
  font-size: 14px;
}
```

Note: this section introduced another new concept for you to understand – making circle divs, and centring divs inside a parent. Hopefully again you were able to decipher the solution yourself, but don't worry if you didn't. These are beyond the realm of a beginner, and are entering the territory of a more intermediate developer. If you did manage to find the solution yourself, fantastic, you are already starting to grow as a developer. One last short section left to style now – the actual content.

Styling the content

This section is not easy and it will test your skills and patience. Keep it up, you're doing great! Now let's finish off our homepage by styling the final part – the content. We're going to keep this simple for now, and simply style the section with a clean white background with dark grey text and a blue headline. White backgrounds are always ideal when dealing with large amounts of text. The clean and high contrast of pairing it with a dark grey allows for increased readability and really helps to reduce eye strain. We always want to ensure nice contrasts between our backgrounds and our text to ensure we maintain a high level of usability. The reason we have opted for dark grey over black text is simple. Black text is actually too much contrast, and proves hard on the eyes. Generally you will want to opt for a dark grey where possible for text as it provides a nice balance between legibility and contrast. Now, let's style this up.

The steps:

Write rules to achieve the following desired output per element:

- #introduction
  - give this element a width of 600px
  - apply a padding all around the element of 20px
  - apply a white background
  - set a solid border around the box of 1px width and make it the colour '#ccc'
  - give the element a margin at the top and bottom of 20px and left and right as automatic
  - give the element rounded corners of 10px radius

- h1
  - apply the colour '#1998E2'
  - give it a font size of 22px
  - align the text in the centre

- p
  - give it a colour of '#777'
  - set the font size to 18px
  - set the line height to 26px

Expected result: once we have written in these rules, we should find that our webpage looks completed, with a nicely centred content element with a larger blue title followed by dark grey text. The entire block should have nicely rounded corners and a border around the lot. The box should also be nicely padded at the edges to improve readability of the text and allow the content to breathe.

Expected code:

```
#introduction {
  width: 600px;
  padding: 20px;
  background: white;
  border: 1px solid #ccc;
  margin: 20px auto;
  border-radius: 10px;
}

h1 {
  color: #1998E2;
  font-size: 22px;
  text-align: center;
}

p {
  color: #777;
  font-size: 18px;
  line-height: 26px;
}
```

Note: congratulations! We just built our homepage together. What a fantastic achievement already. It looks great and it didn't take much code at all. It's a nice, simple and clean website that serves our purpose very well. It's important when designing a website to consider both your audience and also your content. You should adopt the mindset of 'How can we get the most out of our content here?' Let's take this website as an example. This website is going to be information-heavy, text-heavy and its main function is to provide an easy way for us to read back what we have learned. Therefore, we needed to ensure that we created a template that would fit those functions. As a result, we have created a nicely contrasted main content div that ensures ideal line-lengths along with plenty of padding and line height to further improve legibility. We have given the element a middle-ground font size that ensures it can be read, while also allowing us to house a lot of information in a relatively small space. Hopefully you are starting to understand why this layout suits our content so well and maybe you can even spot a few other ways that this layout has considered its audience and content?

Well done again for completing your first webpage. Let's now move on to the HTML page where we can start to build on top of this template.

HTML page

The template

Let's kick things off with updating the page template that we will be using for our actual content pages. We're going to update the template very slightly to assist with the change in information type that we are going to be displaying. We are going to make two changes to the template. First we are going to add in a new method of navigation for our website, which will take the form of a vertical menu, which will be fixed in position so that the users can quickly jump to any section of the page at ease. Second, we are going to replicate the style of our #introduction div into a class, which we will apply to every one of our sections to keep each section separate and also consistent. We will then give each block a unique id which will be used in our jump menu as a bookmark.

HTML

The steps:

- First we will create our new webpage. Create a new file in your root directory and name it 'html.html'.

- Now copy and paste over all of the content from index.html.

- Move the active class in the navigation over to the html link.

- Head down to the introduction div and update the text to the following:

  - Header: HTML

  - Paragraph: 'Welcome to the dedicated HTML section. This page contains all of the HTML elements that I have understood and used so far on my journey into web design' (feel free to alter the text into your own speaking style)

- Now copy the whole #introduction block and paste it directly below the existing one.

- Change the id of the newly pasted block to 'tables' and add on a class to the block of 'section'.

- Update the content as follows:

  - Header: Tables

  - Paragraph: enter here a brief description as per your understanding of tables. Try to write something that you feel will help you to continue to remember and understand them in the future when you come back to this website

- Add a new div underneath the paragraph tag with the class of 'example'.

- Inside the .example div create some example tables for your own reference (feel free to add content to the table or just leave it blank).

- Now just after the .example div, add a button input element with a label of 'Show code' and a class of 'code-show-button'.

Expected result: after carrying out the above steps we should be left with a nice new div which contains a header, paragraph, a table and a button that says 'Show code'. Obviously at this stage it looks pretty ugly, so let's get straight to styling it in the next section.

Expected code:

```html
<!DOCTYPE html>
<html>
<head>
<title>How to build a website</title>
<link rel="stylesheet" href="style.css">
</head>
<body>

<div id="navigation">
 <div id="navigation-inside">
  <ul>
   <li><a href="index.html">Home</a></li>
   <li><a href="html.html" class="active">HTML</a></li>
   <li><a href="css.html">CSS</a></li>
   <li><a href="javascript.html">JavaScript</a></li>
  </ul>
 </div>
</div>

<div id="header">
  <img src="img/header-image.jpg" alt="Header Image">
<div id="profile">
```

```
<div id="profile-image">
<img src="img/profile-icon.png" alt="Profile icon">
</div>
<h2>by<br>Kenny Wood</h2>
</div>
</div>

<div id="introduction">
<h1>HTML</h1>
<p>Welcome to the dedicated HTML section. This page
contains all of the HTML elements that I have understood
and used so far on my journey into web design.</p>
</div>

<div id="tables" class="section">
 <h1>Tables</h1>
 <p>Tables help us to structure data and display it in
  an easy  to digest format.</p>
 <div class="example">
  <table>
   <tr>
    <th>First Column</th>
    <th>Second Column</th>
    <th>Third Column</th>
   </tr>
   <tr>
    <td>Row 1 - Cell 1</td>
    <td>Row 1 - Cell 2</td>
    <td>Row 1 - Cell 3</td>
   </tr>
   <tr>
     <td>Row 2 - Cell 1</td>
     <td>Row 2 - Cell 2</td>
     <td>Row 2 - Cell 3</td>
   </tr>
```

```
  </table>
  </div>
<input class="code-show-button" type="button"
 value="Show code" />
  </div>

</body>
</html>
```

CSS

The goal here is to create a class with the same style as the introduction block, which will be reused on every section we create on our webpages. We will then add a style to highlight the example, before applying a general style to our button to bring it more in line with our webpage style.

The steps:

Write rules to achieve the following desired output per element:

- .section
  - copy and paste the style from the #introduction rule
- .example
  - give this a padding of 10px
  - set the background colour to '#fcfcfc'
  - round the corners off with a radius of 10px to match our containing div
- table
  - set the width to 100%
  - collapse the borders
  - centre all text
- table, th, td
  - set the border to a solid 1px width with the colour #ccc

- . code-show-button
  - – change the inline element into a block
  - – give the top a margin of 20px, left and right automatic margins
  - – apply 10px padding to the top and bottom and 20px to the left and right
  - – give the element rounded corners with a radius of 3px
  - – remove the border that Chrome naturally gives buttons
  - – apply a background colour of '#1998E2'
  - – make the text white
  - – set the font size to 14px
- .code-show-button:hover
  - – change the background to '#198acc'
  - – make the cursor show the 'pointer' finger

Expected result: now doesn't that look better? What you should have now seen is a centred table, sitting inside an example pane of a slightly darker background, followed by a styled button, which says 'show code'.

Expected code:

```css
.section {
  width: 600px;
  padding: 20px;
  background: white;
  border: 1px solid #ccc;
  margin: 20px auto;
  border-radius: 10px;
}
.example {
  padding: 10px;
  background: #fcfcfc;
```

```
    border-radius: 10px;
}

table {
  width: 100%;
  border-collapse: collapse;
  text-align: center;
}
table, th, td {
  border: 1px solid #ccc;
}

.code-show-button {
  display: block;
  margin: 20px auto 0px;
  padding: 10px 20px;
  border-radius: 3px;
  border: none;
  background: #1998E2;
  color: white;
  font-size: 14px;
}

.code-show-button:hover {
  background: #198acc;
  cursor: pointer;
}
```

Note: now in the above challenge, I would be extremely surprised if you managed to get everything right without having to look ahead at the code. There are a lot of new things here that we haven't discussed before. Border collapsing is new to us, as is the button element, styling tables as a whole, not to mention styling the cursor! I'd be downright amazed if you weren't confused or overwhelmed here. But let's quickly break down what we have seen before we move on and create our jump list. So styling tables, yes, it's actually very simple to do. You just use the tag name for the rule (td, tr) and then style it just like you would any other element. The new part here is the border-collapse property. Well, this simply avoids double borders, which would show up if we didn't select the border-collapse property to 'collapse' as table, tr and td all nest within one another. If they all set their borders, we would get lots of double borders. Collapsing the borders merges them into one nice line for us. Next let's tackle the cursor property – this is simple to do. There are a small handful of cursor types we can set on our webpage. We can set them anywhere. In this case we are setting the cursor to change on hover, but we could add it to the body of the page and have it change everywhere. Some examples of the types of cursor we can set are crosshair, grab, move, text, pointer. However, there are many, many more, which you can use at will. In this example we have used the pointer as that is default when hovering over a clickable object. By default our button wasn't showing a pointer cursor, so we had to force the functionality. This is extremely useful as you can turn any element into a button by simply changing the cursor type and attaching some JavaScript to it.

Jump menu

Now that we have our first section, it is a good time for us to create a convenient jump menu to enable us to quickly and easily skip to a certain section in the page with ease. For this we will make use of an unordered list and bookmarks.

HTML

The steps:

- We start by creating the containing div for this menu. So let's create a new div with an id of 'quick-menu', place this div directly below the closing tag of the 'navigation' div.
- Inside the div add an <h3> tag and enter the text 'Quick links'.
- After the closing <h3> tag create an unordered list.
  - add a single list item (for now) with a link to the id for our tables section

Expected result: and that's it for now. Nice and simple. We will obviously be adding to this list with each new section we create, but as far as the HTML structure of this section goes, this is all there is to it. Let's quickly check that your code matches up with mine before we move on to styling the menu.

Expected code:

```
<div id="quick-menu">
<h3>Quick Links</h3>
  <ul>
  <li><a href="#tables">Tables</a></li>
  </ul>
</div>
```

CSS

For the CSS our aim is to create a floating menu that sits just below the main navigation menu, off to the left side of the page, and follows the user down the page as they scroll. Have a think quickly now before moving forward. How do you think we might do this? Give it a go yourself before even looking at the steps. If you are really struggling then feel free to use the steps below, but do try to give it a go yourself first – you might surprise yourself.

The steps:

Write rules to achieve the following desired output per element:

- #quick-menu
    - make the element fixed in position
    - give the element a z-index of a positive number
    - position the element 20px from the left
    - position the element 60px from the top
    - give the element a width of 200px
    - set the height as auto
    - give the element a white background
    - apply 20px of padding to the top and bottom and 10px to either side of the div

- #quick-menu h3
  - remove all margin from the top of the tag
  - align the text in the centre
  - colour the text with #333
  - change the font size to 18px

Expected result: wow, what a difference that makes. We now have a nice and easy way for our users to navigate through our webpage. At any point in the page, no matter how far they scroll, they can always navigate away from the page, or to a different section on the page. This is extremely important with a website like this as it's very likely to have very long pages, once we have added all of our examples. Adding this navigation option enhances the user experience twofold. Remember, we must always consider the user when creating our websites.

Expected code:

```
#quick-menu {
    position: fixed;
    left: 20px;
    top: 60px;
    width: 200px;
    height: auto;
    background: white;
    padding: 20px 10px;
    z-index: 2;
}

#quick-menu h3 {
    margin-top: 0px;
    text-align: center;
    color: #333;
    font-size: 18px;
}
```

Notes: now that we have our jump menu on our page, that leaves just one more aspect to create for our template, before we can start to add our examples into the page and before moving on to the next pages. And that is, of course, the functionality for the 'show code' button. Before we move on to the next section where we will tackle this area of the build, have a little think about how we might do this. Can we show the code with pure CSS and HTML or do we need to add some JavaScript magic? Have a think about how you would also display the code. Would you have it pop up in a prompt for the user to see in isolation? Or would you have a new box appear below the example showing the code? What about once we've clicked the button, how do we get rid of the code again? We don't want to have all of the code on the screen all the time; we will want a way to hide it again otherwise the page could get quite messy very quickly. Have a think about how we should handle this functionality, and then move on to the next section where I will show you how I plan to tackle the challenge. Remember, there is no right or wrong answer here, there are a multitude of ways to do this, and no single one is better or worse than the other. They are simply different ways of tackling the same problem. That's web design for you!

JavaScript

Let's now tackle the problem of showing and hiding our code snippets on our website. So far we have left you to tackle the challenges set on your own, but this section is particularly tricky, so let's walk through it together. If you are feeling confident enough, you are more than welcome to attempt to do this by yourself based on our requirements, which are to show the relevant code to the user. Did you decide how you think it should be done? Well, this is how I plan to do it – hopefully it ties up with how you think we should go about this.

The show button, when clicked, will add a new div below the existing code, which will then show the code on a dark background, then if we click the button again, the div should be removed. We don't want to have to create two divs with the same code in each time we create a new section, so this must be entirely automated and the new div must be generated on the fly.

Let's look in more detail at how we can do this.

We will:

- attach a click handler to our button, which will trigger a function;

- this function will check whether the code example is already on the page or not;

- if it is not on the page, then it will take the code from inside the .example div and spit it back out into a new div below it;

- if the code sample is on the page, then it will remove the div from the page.

Sounds simple enough? Well, let's see what you think in a minute, after we code the functionality.

Let's start by adding our function to our button in our page HTML, like so:

```
<input class="code-show-button" type="button"
onClick="showCode('tables')" value="Show code" />
```

As you can see above, we have added the following code to the element:

```
onClick="showCode('table')"
```

What's happening here is simple. We are passing a function name to be run when the element is clicked. We are passing in the string 'table' into the function. This is because 'table' is the id of the section that we want the new code to show up in. Going forward we will need to update this parameter every time we reuse the snippet in any subsequent sections we create.

Now let's create a new file, which we will call main.js and attach it to our page at the bottom of our body tags.

```
<script src="main.js"></script>
</body>
```

Now we can start to write our showCode() function.

So let's start by declaring it:

```
function showCode(parentElement) {
}
```

Notice how we have created the function and stated that we are expecting a value to be passed in as a parameter, which we are calling 'parentElement'. Remember, when the function is run in our example, the string 'tables' will be passed through here.

Now inside the curly brackets we can start to write the code we want to run when the button is clicked.

Let's start by declaring the variables that we want to make use of inside our function. For this function we will first want a reference to the parent div of the section, which will house the new content. We will also want a reference to the element that contains the code for our new div, which in this case is the '.example' div.

```
var parentElementDiv = document.getElementById(parent
Element);
var exampleElement = document.querySelector('#' +
parentElement + '.example');
```

Let's talk a bit about what just happened here. So we declared a variable named 'parentElementDiv' and assigned it to the result of a function named getElementById, which was called from the document object. The document object simply references everything we can see on our webpage. It is literally the webpage document. The getElementById method that we are calling, will search through the document (webpage) and look for an element with the id that we pass to it. In this case, it will find the element with the 'tables' id. (Notice how we don't need to specify the # to denote id here as it is already expecting an id anyway.)

Then we declared a new variable named 'exampleElement', which contains the result of the method querySelector(), which is also run from the document object. This function works a bit differently. It's similar to how we specify elements in CSS. We pass in a query to find the element we are looking for. In this case, because we only want the '.example' div that sits inside of the parent that we passed in, we need to nest it inside the parent's element, just like we would in CSS. You will notice here that we do need to add '.' and '#' to our query, just like we would in CSS to ensure that we get the result we are looking for.

Now that we have our variables, we can start to make use of them.

Let's next perform the relevant check to see if the code is already shown on the webpage or not. We can do this by checking for the existence of a class on the parent element that we passed in. Basically we are going to add a class of 'open' to the parent div when we click the 'show code' button. This way we have a clear indicator that the code is being shown. So let's detect this in an if statement.

```
if(parentElementDiv.className === 'section open') {
} else {
}
```

More new code here, so let's step through it again. We are looking at the variable we assigned at the top of our function, and picking off the property 'className' from it, which will return the classes added to the element. In our HTML we specified that the element has a class of 'section' so we need to be aware of this when we write our conditional statement for our if statement. In our code above we are detecting whether the element has the classes 'section' and 'open' assigned to it. If it does, then it will run the first set of braces, if not (else) it will run the next block of code. So let's work first on the case where it does not have the open class, and therefore needs to show the code in the new div.

So what we're going to do here is as follows. We are going to assign a variable to the content of the '.example' div, then we are going to create a new div, and pass in the content. We're going to give it an id of 'example-code', then we're going to update the text of the button to say 'Hide code', then finally we're going to add the class 'open' to the main section div to highlight that the code is exposed. Let's look at the code for this.

```
var text = exampleElement.innerHTML;
var code = document.createTextNode(text);
var codeElement = document.createElement('div');
codeElement.appendChild(code);
codeElement.className = 'example-code';
exampleElement.appendChild(codeElement);
document.querySelector('#' + parentElement + '.code-
show-button').value = "Hide code";
parentElementDiv.classList.add('open');
```

Let's step through this code to understand exactly what each of these methods and properties does for us.

We first set up a variable to contain the code that we want to put in a separate div:

```
// Sets a variable to the content of the exampleElement
element
    var text = exampleElement.innerHTML;
```

We then create a 'text node' from that content and assign it to a variable named 'code'. We won't go into too much detail about what a text node is, but in short, it is the text inside an element on our webpage.

```
// Creates the text that we want to use into a 'text
node' which can then be added to an element
   var code = document.createTextNode(text);
```

After we have our text node, we create a new div element, pass in our code snippet (text node) as a child (which will then become the content of the div), we then give this newly created div an id of 'example-code'.

```
// Creates a new div element and assigns it to a
variable
var codeElement = document.createElement('div');

// Enter the text node into our element
   codeElement.appendChild(code);

// And give our element a class of 'example-code'
codeElement.className = 'example-code';
```

Once we have our new element stored as a variable, we pass this element to our exampleElement object, which, remember, is a reference to the '.example' div.

```
// Pass the newly created element into the
exampleElement (our .example div)
exampleElement.appendChild(codeElement);
```

Now that our code is showing up in our new div, we then change the text of the button to let the user know that the action of the button has changed, then, finally we add an 'open' class to the main '.section' div to highlight that we are showing code inside this block.

```
// Change the text of the button to 'Hide code'
document.querySelector('#' + parentElement + '.code-
show-button').value = "Hide code";
// Add the class 'open' to our main parent element
parentElementDiv.classList.add('open');
```

Now that we have created our JavaScript for when we want to open up our new div, we need to write the other side of the if statement, responsible for getting rid of the element once the user clicks the 'hide code' button.

Fortunately, this is a bit simpler than the code to create the div in the first place.

All we really need to do here is provide a reference to our newly created element, then remove it from the parent node, before changing the button text back to 'Show code' and removing the 'open' class from the main div.

Once again, let's look at the code for this before stepping through this final part of the puzzle.

```
var codeBlock = exampleElement.querySelector('.example-
code');
exampleElement.removeChild(codeBlock);
document.querySelector('#' + parentElement + ' .code-
show-button').value = "Show code";
parentElementDiv.classList.remove('open');
```

See, not so bad. Just four fairly simple statements. Let's go through them now.

We start by declaring a variable and assigning it to the '.example-code' div we created when we clicked the button to show the code.

```
// search the exampleElement object for the '.example-
code' class and assign it to codeBlock
var codeBlock = exampleElement.querySelector('.example-
code');
```

We then remove this codeBlock element from its parent.

```
// Remove the code block from the webpage
exampleElement.removeChild(codeBlock);
```

Finishing up, we then set the buttons text back to 'Show code' and then remove the 'open' div class from our parent element.

```
// Change the buttons text back to 'Show code'
document.querySelector('#' + parentElement + '.code-
show-button').value = "Show code";
// Remove the 'open' div from the parent
   parentElementDiv.classList.remove('open');
```

If we now put this all back together, we end up with this:

```
function showCode(parentElement) {
  var parentElementDiv = document.
  getElementById(parentElement);
  var exampleElement = document.querySelector('#' +
  parentElement + '.example')

  if(parentElementDiv.className == 'section open') {
  var codeBlock = exampleElement.querySelector('.
  example-code');
  exampleElement.removeChild(codeBlock);
  document.querySelector('#' + parentElement + '.code-show-
  button').value = "Show code";
  parentElementDiv.classList.remove('open');
```

```
} else {
  var text = exampleElement.innerHTML;
  var code = document.createTextNode(text);
  var codeElement = document.createElement('div');
  codeElement.appendChild(code);
  codeElement.className = 'example-code';
  exampleElement.appendChild(codeElement);
  document.querySelector('#' + parentElement + '.code-show-
  button').value = "Hide code";
  parentElementDiv.classList.add('open');
}
}
```

Now all that's left to do is to write the single CSS rule for our '.example-code' div.

For this I will now hand control back over to you to complete this task. Head over to your 'main.css' file and write the following rules for the property '.example-code':

- A background of #333.
- Text colour of white.
- Padding of 10px.
- Rounded corners with a radius of 10px.
- 20px margin from the top of the div.

If you coded this correctly, you should end up with the following code:

```
.example-code {
  background: #333;
  color: white;
  padding: 10px;
  border-radius: 10px;
  margin-top: 20px;
}
```

Our page template has now been created. From here on in it's just a case of adding in the various sections and creating the subsequent pages from the same template. Congratulations on getting through this section. I know the JavaScript section we just looked at must have been particularly difficult, even if there wasn't the expectation to work out the solution yourself. The section introduced a lot of new methods and properties and introduced some concepts and logic that we haven't seen before. I know this might seem a bit overwhelming at first, but once it's broken down and you work through it line by line, it becomes much easier to understand. Even if you are still struggling with what exactly is happening, don't worry – that example is a bit more advanced than a typical beginner exercise; however, it's important that we have the more advanced code in our website to provide you with a goal to work towards with your understanding of JavaScript. Not to mention it also allows us the great functionality of being able to quickly and easily peek into the source code behind the examples that we are going to write into our website.

The JavaScript example also perfectly highlights how JavaScript can take your website to the next level of user experience. We now have a highly useful functionality piece on our website that we coded once, and can be used everywhere very easily. Now, instead of copying and pasting the code of our examples into another div

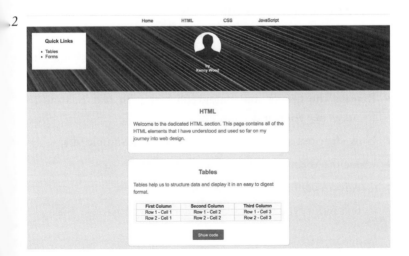

directly into the HTML, and having to do that for each and every example we write, we can simply change the string we pass into our click event handler, and the JavaScript will handle the rest for us. Just imagine how much time this has just saved us!

Right, now that we have our template file completed, let's fill it with our content! The plan here is for this website to become your personal log of all the HTML, CSS and JavaScript that you have encountered and understand. Once we have finished our journey together, you then have a complete reference to every-thing web design related that you have encountered, which you can continue to update as you journey deeper and deeper into the rabbit hole of web design. Let's start some of these examples to-gether before you go off on your own and finish off the page by yourself.

Forms

We're going to create a very simple web form that allows the user to input some information, and then provides a prompt that the form was submitted if the user clicks the submit button.

The steps:

- Copy the entire block of code we created for the tables section and paste it directly underneath the existing tables section.
- Replace the blocks id with 'forms'.
- Replace the onClick method's parameter value from 'tables' to 'forms'.
- Replace the header and paragraph text with text relating to forms as per your understanding.
- Now clear out all of the content inside the '.example' div.
- Inside the '.example' div add the following:
  - A form containing the following:

    text input type with a placeholder value of 'name'

another text input type with a placeholder value of 'email'

a submit input with the value 'Submit'

- Now make the form show an alert box saying 'Form was submitted' when the submit button is clicked.

Expected result: so here, as with the previous sections, there are a couple of points in the list that we haven't seen before. Just like with the previous examples, in this case, you should try your best to work out yourself how to overcome these obstacles using Google. If you are still struggling, then read on to see the solution.

Expected code:

```
<div id="forms" class="section">
  <h1>Forms</h1>
  <p>Forms allow us to collect an input from a user and
    perform an action with their input.</p>
  <div class="example">
  <form onsubmit="return alert('Form was submitted!')"
    method="post">
    <input type="text" name="name" placeholder="name"><br>
    <input type="text" name="mail" placeholder="email"><br>
    <input type="submit" value="Submit">
    </form>
  </div>
  <input class="code-show-button" type="button"
  onClick="showCode('forms')" value="Show code" />
  </div>
```

Note: as you can see from the above code, we have entered some simple JavaScript right into the 'onsubmit' attribute of the form opening tag. This is a great way to run simple operations on a web form. If you have checked out your website in the browser after adding this section, you might have noticed that the form is looking quite bland. Let's improve the look and feel with some very simple CSS rules.

CSS

Head on over to your CSS file and add the following rule under the following property 'form, input[type=text], input[type=submit]':

- Width of 300px.
- A margin of 5px at the top and bottom and automatic at the sides.
- Padding of 10px.

Save your file and check out how it looks in your browser. You might notice a small quirk appearing to destroy the layout of our form. The boxes are being made bigger than our input button. This is because of the type of sizing we have applied to our elements. Let's change that now with one simple rule in our CSS.

```
div {
  box-sizing: border-box;
}
```

Give the file a save and refresh your browser. Everything should line up perfectly now.

Right now you are probably thinking 'What's a border box?' Well, the box-sizing property is a way of telling the browser how to handle our height and width values. By default, the box has a 'content-box' sizing, which means that border, padding and margin are not included inside the fixed width that we have set on our inputs. If we change the value to 'border-box' everything is included within the width, which can really help with our layout. You might have noticed that all of our divs on our webpage are suddenly slightly smaller, this is a good thing and shows that our code has worked as expected. By adding this rule into our CSS we are less likely to get tripped by with any other sizing issues down the line.

Our newly added CSS rules should look like so:

```
form, input[type=text], input[type=submit] {
 width: 300px;
 margin: 5px auto;
 padding: 10px;
}
div {
 box-sizing: border-box;
}
```

There's just one last thing left to do for this section now, and that is to add a new link to the quick links menu referencing our new 'forms' section. This one is nice and simple, and once you've made the change your quick links should look just like this:

```
<div id="quick-menu">
<h3>Quick Links</h3>
<ul>
<li><a href="#tables">Tables</a></li>
<li><a href="#forms">Forms</a></li>
</ul>
</div>
```

Conclusion

Right, I think that marks the end of this webpage for me. For you, though, the job is not finished yet. You should now go through the HTML section of this book again, adding all the HTML examples and concepts that you find along the way to your website. Some examples of things you could add to the webpage are as follows:

- images (why not create a mini photo gallery);
- links;
- unordered lists;

- ordered lists;
- div class;
- div id; and
- spans.

It's a good idea to do this now as it will test your knowledge and understanding of what we have learned so far. At this point you should have a solid grasp of visual design and should be able to add in examples of each of the above elements while updating the styles accordingly to ensure it looks good and fits in with our current style. The training wheels are off now, go and see what you can create. When you are ready, let's move on to the CSS page and we can start you off with a couple more CSS examples over there. Keep going, you are doing great!

CSS page

Hopefully now you have had a chance to go through and finish off the HTML page with more examples. Great stuff, let's now turn our focus to the CSS page and jump straight in with a few examples of how we can show our examples on this page. Let's first get started with the base file.

The steps:

- Let's take our html.html page and duplicate it to css.html.
- Now make all of the necessary changes to turn it into the CSS page:
  - change the title
  - change the active class on the navbar
  - strip out the section divs – leave one for us to use as a template
  - rewrite the introductory text
  - remove all of the quick links we added

Great, now we should have a nice base file to work from.

Let's go straight in with an example of styling text. This is going to be nice and simple. All we are going to do is:

- Edit the '.section' div that you left when you were migrating html.html to css.html.

- Add a new title and paragraph for styling text.

- Add a relevant id to the section and replicate the id down in the click handler function value.

- Add a link to the quick links navigation menu with the id as the ref value.

- Inside the '.example' div create a paragraph tag with some text inside it.

- Now add the following style directly to the paragraph opening tag:

  - change the colour of the text to '#1998E2'

  - change the font size to anything of your choosing

  - alter the line height

  - change the alignment

  - add in any other text styles you deem appropriate

Now save the file and check out the file in the browser. You should see your text with the styling you applied to it. Clicking the 'show code' button should show the inline styles code you used to make the changes to the text's style.

The code for this page should look like this:

```
<!DOCTYPE html>
<html>
<head>
<title>How to build a website</title>
<link rel="stylesheet" href="style.css">
</head>
<body>
```

```
<div id="navigation">
 <div id="navigation-inside">
  <ul>
   <li><a href="index.html">Home</a></li>
   <li><a href="html.html">HTML</a></li>
   <li><a href="css.html" class="active">CSS</a></li>
   <li><a href="javascript.html">JavaScript</a></li>
  </ul>
 </div>
</div>

<div id="quick-menu">
<h3>Quick Links</h3>
<ul>
<li><a href="#styling-text">Styling Text</a></li>
</ul>
</div>

<div id="header">
  <img src="img/header-image.jpg" alt="Header Image">
<div id="profile">
<div id="profile-image">
<img src="img/profile-icon.png" alt="Profile icon">
</div>
<h2>by<br>Kenny Wood</h2>
</div>
</div>

<div id="introduction">
<h1>CSS</h1>
<p>Welcome to the dedicated CSS section. This page
contains all of the CSS properties that I have
understood and used so far on my journey into web
design.</p>
</div>

<div id="styling-text" class="section">
  <h1>Styling Text</h1>
```

```
    <p>Styling text is an important part of web design as
it allows us to ensure that text is legible and also
fits in with the style of the webpage.</p>
    <div class="example">
<p style="color: #1998E2; font-size: 16px; line-height:
18px; text-align: center;">This is my example of some
styled text</p>
    </div>
    <input class="code-show-button" type="button"
onClick="showCode('styling-text')" value="Show code" />
    </div>

<script src="main.js"></script>
</body>
</html>
```

Next steps

Now that we have created this example of how we can demonstrate our understanding of CSS, you are free again to go off and add in the rest of the properties that you have an understanding of. Go back through the CSS chapter of this book and add sections for all of the different CSS properties that you encounter. Then, just like we did with the HTML page, we will have a full catalogue of all of our code snippets that we can refer back to later. Once you have finished updating this page, move on to the next section where we will be building the final page of our website, the JavaScript page.

Conclusion

Congratulations. You're one step closer to completing your first reference website. It's really coming together nicely now. Each web-page is slightly different, yet still maintains the overall style of the website. This is the goal when creating websites. We want uniform-ity among all of our pages, even when the design is slightly different across the various pages. Now on to the final page of our website.

JavaScript page

So here we are. The final page. You are about to complete your first website. This website uses three different languages to achieve its desired output. I bet you didn't think you'd have an understanding of three separate languages and be able to put them all together seamlessly to create a website so soon into your web design career.

Right, let's get going with the JavaScript page. Just like with the CSS page, we are going to maintain the same template, but make some slight adjustments to how we demonstrate the code example inside our '.example' div.

The steps:

- Let's take our html.html page and duplicate it to javascript.html.

- Now make all of the necessary changes to turn it into the JavaScript page:

  - change the title

  - change the active class on the navbar

  - strip out the section divs – leave one for us to use as a template

  - rewrite the introductory text

  - remove all of the quick links we added

Now we should have a nice base file to work from again.

Let's go straight in with an example of a JavaScript function. We're going to start with a nice and simple for loop. With these functions, the description of each function is going to be hugely important as the output won't always mean a lot to the user without some context as to how we got to the output.

- Edit the '.section' div that you left when you were migrating html.html to javascript.html.

- Add a new title and paragraph for 'for loops'.

- Add a relevant id to the section and replicate the id down in the click handler function value.

- Add a link to the quick links navigation menu with the id as the ref value.

- Inside the '.example' div create a pair of script tags.
- Inside the script tags write a for statement which:
  - loops 10 times and logs to the console the number of the variable each time it runs
  - wrap this loop in a function
- Create an input button and pass the function we just created to the onClick event handler.
- Add a class of 'run-javascript' to the button.

Now save the file and check out the file in the browser. You should see the button inside, which, when clicked outputs 1,2,3,4,5,6, 7,8,9,10 to the console. Clicking 'Show code' should show the whole script tag and its contents.

The button looks a bit uninspired, so let's update the style of the button to make it look a bit more exciting. Head over to your CSS file and add the following rules for the '.run-javascript' class:

- Margin top and bottom of 0px, left and right margin of automatic.
- A width of 200px.
- Change the display type to a block.

Now our button should be a bit bigger and centred. Much better. Now we have a working snippet of JavaScript attached to a button, the code of which can easily be viewed by clicking the 'show code' button. Perfect! Before we wrap this page up, let's quickly check that we have the same code written.

Expected code:

```
<!DOCTYPE html>
<html>
<head>
<title>How to build a website</title>
<link rel="stylesheet" href="style.css">
</head>
<body>
```

```
<div id="navigation">
 <div id="navigation-inside">
  <ul>
   <li><a href="index.html">Home</a></li>
   <li><a href="html.html">HTML</a></li>
   <li><a href="css.html">CSS</a></li>
   <li><a href="javascript.html" class="active">
    JavaScript</a></li>
  </ul>
 </div>
</div>

<div id="quick-menu">
<h3>Quick Links</h3>
<ul>
<li><a href="#for-loop">for loop</a></li>
</ul>
</div>

<div id="header">
  <img src="img/header-image.jpg" alt="Header Image">
<div id="profile">
<div id="profile-image">
<img src="img/profile-icon.png" alt="Profile icon">
</div>
<h2>by<br>Kenny Wood</h2>
</div>
</div>

<div id="introduction">
<h1>JavaScript</h1>
<p>Welcome to the dedicated JavaScript section. This
page contains all of the JavaScript elements that I
have understood and used so far on my journey into web
design.</p>
</div>
```

```
<div id="for-loop" class="section">
  <h1>for loop</h1>
<p>for loops are great for getting a statement to run a
certain number of times. In the below example, clicking
the button will start a for loop which will run exactly
10 times and log to the console each time</p>
  <div class="example">
<script>
function runForLoop() {
for( var i = 1; i <= 10; i++ ) {
console.log("This loop has run " + i + " times");
}
}
</script>
<input type="button" class="run-javascript" value="Run
for loop" onclick="runForLoop()" />
</div>

  <input class="code-show-button" type="button"
onClick="showCode('for-loop')" value="Show code" />
</div>
<script src="main.js"></script>
</body>
</html>
```

Next steps

Just like with the HTML and CSS sections, it is now up to you to go through the JavaScript section in this book and add new sections for each example of an area of JavaScript that you encounter. Some examples that I can suggest for this would be:

- math operations;
- string methods;
- objects;

- arrays;
- switch statement;
- if statements;
- the do/while loop.

Conclusion

Well there we have it, you've just finished creating your first website. At the start of this book, we introduced how websites work, and here we are at the end and you have just finished creating your own website from scratch. Your resilience and determination will serve you well as a web designer – these traits are an essential part of being successful in the ever-evolving field. Congratulations again for sticking it out and getting to the end of the book. However, now that we have created our website, there is just one tiny thing left to do. Get it online. In the final chapter of this book, we will take your website from a folder on your computer to having its own URL, accessible from all over the world.

Possible further improvements

Just one quick note before we leave this section and get your website online. While this website is built, like everything in web design, nothing is ever truly finished as we can always improve our website further. If you want to take your website to the next level and use some more advanced techniques, then here is a small list of possible enhancements that you could make to the website:

- *Optimization.* A fast website will serve you well and help hugely with ensuring your users have a pleasant time browsing. There's a plethora of tweaks we can make to our website to enhance performance. Why not do some research into the current trends for optimizing websites? This is an ever-evolving aspect of programming, so who knows what's popular at the time of reading this.

- *Create a favicon for your website.* Ever seen those small icons that sit to the far left of your tab showing the logo of the website you're on? These are called favicons. Why not create one for your website? They will also be used when a user bookmarks your website.

- *Update the quick links to be dynamic.* Why not update the static quick links menu we have on each page to dynamically populate on page load, based on the content of the page? A bit of JavaScript could take care of this fairly easily and will remove the monotonous task of updating it manually every time you add a new section.

- *Mobile-friendly.* This one is hugely important, but also quite tricky to understand. It could almost be another book in itself, but you can pick the basics up fairly quickly. Responsive web design is the current, most popular way of making your website mobile friendly. Check out some tutorials online and update your website for all screen sizes!

12
Getting your website online

In the last chapter, we created a website together from scratch, through to a beautiful, useful encyclopaedia of our knowledge of web design. At the moment it is a hugely useful tool for you to use whenever you are on your computer, but what about when you are not at your computer, what if you were at a different machine, how would you access the website then? Websites belong online – it's that simple – so let's get your website up and on to the internet with the rest of them.

Domains and hosting

So, to get our site up and running, we need two things. We need a domain and a hosting service. For our simplistic needs at this stage, we can combine both of these with using a service like godaddy.com. At GoDaddy (or similar) you are able to buy the domain of your choice and then optionally set up a hosting package too. Hosting is simply paying for space on a server that will 'host' and 'serve' your website.

I will leave it to you to go ahead and choose your registrar, to register your domain and set up hosting, and then once you have, you should be given some information about accessing your hosting storage. Typically you will be given an FTP login. If you recall right from the very first chapter of this book, FTP is a method of

12.1

exchanging files with a server. Once we have our FTP details, we can get our website online.

To do this we need to install and open an FTP client. For the purposes of this book, we will be using an application called FileZilla. It is free software and exists across all modern platforms (macOS and Windows, etc).

Let's open up FileZilla now and log in to our hosting service.

When you open up FileZilla you will be greeted with the screen shown in Figure 12.1.

What you are looking at on the left-hand side is a directory of your computer. Start by navigating through to where you have your website files located and enter that directory on the source tree. You should then see the list of files in the pane, as shown in Figure 12.2.

12.2

Once we have navigated to our folder, we can login with our FTP details. To do this you can simply use the 'Quickconnect' toolbar at the top (Figure 12.3).

12.3

Here you can enter the FTP details that you should have received from your registrar upon obtaining your domain and hosting.

Once we have entered our details and clicked 'Quickconnect', the right pane will update to show the folder structure of the server to which we have just connected.

Typically the details that you are provided from your hosting package will restrict your access to any folder other than the folder responsible for your website, so you will instantly be taken to the

12.4

'web folder'. However, if you have a full server directory, you will want to navigate to the following folder /var/www/html. This is where the server will be looking for your website files.

Now we can simply select all of the files on the left, which make up our website, and drag and drop them over to the right-hand side, and thus, onto our server. And that's pretty much it! Our website should now be ready to view at the chosen domain name, which will naturally redirect to the index.html file as the default homepage for our website.

Yes, it's really that simple to get a website online. Surprising, right?

Just a quick note before we wrap up. If your site does not show up, you could have a permissions error. In this case you will need to select all of your files in the RIGHT pane and right-click on them, then go to 'file permissions'. This will open up a new dialogue box. In here you will see a text box with some numbers in it. Type the number 755 and ensure the option 'recurse into subdirectories' is checked and set to 'apply to all files and directories'. Click ok and wait for the permissions to be updated. This should fix this issue. It's important to note that if you ever build more complex websites, with a back-end service, the deployment process is vastly different to this, so please do check the most appropriate permissions for your specific setup.

Conclusion

And there we have it – our website is online! Now, remember that every time we make a change to our website, we need to upload the new files to the server again in order to reflect our change on our website. This process will become second nature in no time at all. Let's close this chapter out by paying attention to what we just achieved. We just published our first website together! This is a big moment – you have now created something of value and sent it out into the world where anyone can see it. Now imagine for a second the world of possibilities that have just opened up to you now that you understand how to build static websites. Well done again for your hard work and progress through this book. It's not easy to get this far and you have made it out the other side and actually published your website. You should give yourself a big pat on the back and rest assured that you're already following in the footsteps of many great developers by showing grit and determination to stick it out and learn three new languages all in the space of one book. That's impressive stuff, right there. Well done!

Conclusion

This is the end. Only, it's not really ever the end with web design. If you're still thirsty for more there's always advanced techniques, changes in the field, progressive web apps, mobile support, touch support, VR and augmented reality to consider, web games to build, servers to configure, build tools, server-side scripting or databases to be getting on with, isn't there? Welcome to web design – the industry where you will never know everything there is to know, and as soon as you think you do know everything you need to know, the landscape changes and evolves and you are thrust back into learning a new language, technique or tool to improve the website building experience. But isn't that all part of the fun? Imagine if that was it – you read this book, and instantly you were an expert in the field and never had to learn anything web related again. A builder can learn to build a brick wall, and never have to learn it again. By contrast, a web developer can finish learning one aspect of web design, for it to be outdated and no longer best practice a week later. Becoming a good web developer is about reading the tea leaves of the industry; understanding what direction things are heading, and jumping on board at the right time with the new technologies that emerge every day in the field.

This is exactly what this book has prepared you for.

The single most important trait a web developer can have is resilience. The ability to tough it out during those moments where you think to yourself 'I have no idea how to solve this problem.' By getting to the end of this book, you have proved to both yourself and me that you have what it takes to make it in this industry. Even if you choose to not continue your path into web design, the skills you have picked up from this book will be incredibly valuable to you going forward. The logical way that your brain has had to work in order to complete the exercises is hugely beneficial for when you come face to face with a problem again in the future, web related or not.

I take my hat off to you, as I know web design can be a huge pain at times, and it really is full of strange quirks, but that's what I have learned to love about it over the years, and hopefully you are starting to feel the same way. I know this book must have been a big challenge for you, but I sincerely hope you have enjoyed the journey and found it as exciting and interesting as the day when I first introduced myself to web design. Hopefully I have managed to instil in you the same passion and curiosity that took me over on that day and has remained with me ever since.

Good luck with your future in web design. You truly have picked a fantastic field to journey through. I struggle to think of any job more rewarding and satisfying than web design.

Thank you for choosing my book as the one to have the pleasure of introducing you into this wonderful world. Now go off and build something revolutionary!

INDEX